Women Elders *Speak*

Reflecting on the pandemic

Library of Congress Cataloging-in-Publication Data on file.

ISBN 978-1-71-549759-0

General Editor: Jayne Maginot
Executive Editor: Jo Anne Salisbury Troxel
Graphic Design: Marcia Rueter Leritz
Last page and Susan Wickland image from Freepik.com
Cover design: Allison Troxel
Illustration on Front Cover: Alexander, Nina. *As an Antidote to Death, I Eat the Stars*. 2020. Pastel on paper. 19" x 25".

Featured Writers and Images: Susan Backer, Faye Boom, Dorothy Bradley, Collette Brooks-Hops, Glen Chamberlain, Jessie Close, Susie Cole, Mary E. Costello, Betsy Danforth, Jean Davis, Mallery Downs, Teresa Durrant, Mary Beth Green, Sue Gust, Jane Jelinski, Joy LaClaire, Terry Lankutis, Kimberlee Lawrence, D Jan Matney, Jackie Montgomery, Susan Morgan, Mary R. Nelson, Pamela Niemi, Joni Payne, Carolyn Pinet, Adele Pittendrigh, Marcia Prather, Jane Quinn, Marcia Rueter Leritz, June Safford, Kelly L. Simmons, Beth Sirr, Nancy Slabaugh Hart, Kathy Springmeyer, Jo Anne Salisbury Troxel, Mattie Whitehouse, Susan Wickland, Sara Williams, Jill Woodworth, Tracy Woodworth
Featured Artists: Collette Brooks-Hops

Printed and Bound in The United States of America
First Printing January 2021

CONTENTS

In every crisis, doubt or confusion,
take the higher path—the path of compassion,
courage, understanding and love.
—Amit Ray

Foreword

Women Elders Speak is the latest book project from third generation Montanan and Bozeman octogenarian Jo Anne Salisbury Troxel. This now retired English teacher was known by her students to enjoy challenging them to think in new ways. A teacher to her core, her peppery spirit is like a flare in the night sky, an invitation to add beauty, to connect, and offer the light of hope to these dark and difficult days.

Jo Anne's contagious spirit inspires individuals to act and speak out and this book is a testament to her effectiveness. Together Jo Anne with her dear friend, a friend who thinks very differently from her, Dr. Marcia Prather, contacted women in their inner circles with a simple request: share your experience of the 2020 Spring Pandemic.

Forty-two women responded to their call and I've had the pleasure of interacting with nearly all of them. This is their book.

Compiling and editing *Women Elders Speak* has been a fun and challenging undertaking made much simpler and more delightful thanks to the talents of veteran graphic designer, Marcia Rueter Leritz, who kindly offered her assistance early in the editing process.

Lastly, a sincere thank you to every one who contributed their time and effort to make this book a reality. Writing is not easy. Being vulnerable is not easy. Putting in your best effort is not easy. It is, however, appreciated. So thank you.

Enjoy.

Jayne Maginot
Writer, Editor
Bozeman, Montana

Introduction

March 11, 2020. My daughter Allison and her partner, Cindy, come in the back door loaded with groceries, and tell me I am in quarantine. They are well-informed about COVID-19 and know that I am vulnerable being 86 years old. They assure me they will bring groceries, and cook extra food for me. At that moment, they are keeping a 6-foot distance, and wearing masks. Filial piety is gratifying receiving such respect; in exchange, I listen to them, for it is all very doable.

I alphabetize the spice shelves: Allspice to Yarrow; sort through dresser drawers tossing everything over ten years old; cull the book shelves of philosophy, psychology, and literary anthologies; make decisions about sleeveless unworn dresses, blouses, short skirts, all once favorites. Now, at 86, I am a changed person, and those clothes belonged to someone else.

Now what? I am feeling sad, restless, uneasy.

April 13, 2020. I have been in quarantine for a month, and it is hitting me hard that this could go on a long time. The amount of deaths in New York alone was staggering. "You need a project," Allison said. She continued to make her point, "You mentioned once something about having older women talk about being sequestered. You need to do this. You're finding this time, without easy access to your friends, your old habits, like a little death of your expectations, your life."

I wondered what it was like for other older women. That same day, I called my friend, Dr. Marcia Prather, and we discussed what I had in mind, and she agreed to help. She has many friends, some in the medical field, whom she agreed to contact. We began immediately. The women we contacted were eager to participate.

April 15, 2020. After five weeks in quarantine, and understanding it may go on for an indefinite period of time, these women were experiencing their lives in new and surprising ways. This is why I was interested in these first, unique impressions, before the pandemic went on for so long and we became inured to the crises and death around us; before we became resigned, and tolerant.

I sent out a brief suggestion sheet to all the women we contacted. It was simple. With a due date of May 20, 2020, write 400 to 1,200 words, talk about what you are experiencing in this time. Amazingly enough, most of these 40 entries came in on schedule, with a few revising until June.

When my daughter Allison had to have a procedure on her shoulder, and was unable to continue editing and organizing this project, we asked Jayne Maginot, writer and editor, if she would take over. Right up her expertise alley, painstaking about form and content, she has done the astonishing job you see here. Jayne was a joy to work with, and was ever ready with suggestions, observations, and rare insights. Graphic designer Marcia Rueter Leritz' genius melded the fetching graphics of photos to articles. The unusual and beautiful cover of this book is a drawing by local artist and friend, Nina Alexander. She was inspired by a poem by Rebecca Elson, (1960–1999) *As an Antidote to Fear of Death, I Eat the Stars*.

They all helped make this book not only an inspirational read, but an artistic endeavor honoring the women writers that share their intimate thoughts with us, the curious and interested stranger.

I am grateful for the wide response to this project from women from not only Bozeman, but from all over Montana and the United States. They have spoken truth to their experience with so much awareness of this special time that we, the reader, will find ourselves in these pages.

Jo Anne Salisbury Troxel
Writer, social activist
Bozeman, Montana

One View from the Pandemic
by Susan Backer

Born in 1947 in Crookston, Minnesota,
Susan Backer is a retired Elementary Teacher and
an active leader in the Unitarian Universalist Fellowship
and lives in Bozeman, Montana.

I am writing this on Memorial Day Weekend 2020 when Montana is slowly opening up after having been closed to all but essential services since late March. I arrived home in Bozeman on March 10th from a short trip to visit a friend in Sun City, Arizona and family in San Diego, California. Keeping apprised of the news, I realized that I would need to go into self-quarantine since I'd been in two communities and on several flights.

The first weeks of isolation didn't bother me. Having been widowed for almost five years, I have been steadily working on becoming accustomed to living alone with my two small dogs. I have wide interests and good social connections. So I learned how to participate in Zoom meetings, and I was lay leader for one of the early-streamed services of my fellowship. I visited with friends and families on the phone and found out which grocery stores would deliver. However, once I had gotten through some household chore lists, read the pile of books set aside for "a rainy day" and completed one too many jigsaw puzzles by myself. I started to get serious cabin fever. I was acutely missing the physical presence of others.

I am no stranger to solitude and in fact have actively sought it at different times throughout my life. For thirty-five years, my husband,

Marv, and I lived in Bear Canyon just outside of Bozeman, where we could be hermits when we wanted to be. There's the catch: when we wanted to be. Sometimes living in these times with COVID-19 reminds me a bit of living in that mountain canyon. We always knew the bears were there. We just didn't know where, or when, we'd run into them.

During these months, I was also gravely concerned and overwhelmed with caring for my older dog, Abby, who had been ill off-and-on throughout the winter and appeared to be going into a decline. Taking her to the vet for evaluation and treatment, I handed her through the opened car window to a masked and gowned technician, but wasn't allowed to go in with her. That was a turning point in my emotional steadiness as my little companion couldn't have the person closest to her holding and supporting her. That's when it truly sunk in that life had drastically changed. That's when I realized how much I was missing and needing my friends and family. I needed my community.

The importance of community is easy to forget when we're in a position to take it for granted. Seasons have come and gone in my life, but for the past forty-some years the Unitarian Universalist Fellowship has been my closest community, my chosen family, and my deepest commitment.

Since mid-March, on Sunday mornings now, I go to my den and turn on the computer to participate in our streaming services. As the minister lights the chalice, I light my own on the table beside me. I sing along with the hymns, listen to the sermon, and hear the Joys and Concerns that the minister has received from congregants. But it's definitely not the same as being physically in the church. I miss the hugs, the handshakes, and the arms about the shoulders as we interact and share our lives with each other.

Some Sundays for the streaming service I leave the video on so my picture is on the side of the screen with other participants. Sometimes I can't do that because I'm feeling vulnerable, and know that scenes of the empty sanctuary with the deeply meaningful altar screens and the words and melodies of the hymns will bring tears. The altar screens in particular bring back so many memories of the folks who designed them, contributed fabric, and helped to make them. Those screens were a grounding identity for our fellowship as we moved from rental space to rental space over the years. What a great irony it is now, that after working decades to have our own building, finally acquired in 2015, at our beautiful sanctuary space stands empty.

I know that I am one of the lucky ones. I don't have to worry about going to work or where my next paycheck is coming from. I'm living in one of the safest—so far—states in the nation. But I am very concerned about family members and dear friends living in states and countries where the virus is rampant. I worry about graduates across our nation who have not been able to celebrate their accomplishments, and who may not have a job to enter now. I worry about the futures of my great-nephews and my cousins' children. I know younger folks in my fellowship who had started businesses that were closed , classified as non-essential. What happens with their bank loans, the rental due for their spaces . . . and more? I am worried about the politicization of a disease and how it has polarized our country even further than it was before. How do we move forward?

In a mask in the vet's office, when I knew my little companion's suffering had become too much , and the only loving thing I could do was to have her put down, I was able to be with her. As I stroked and talked to her in her final moments, I wished she could have seen my familiar face without the mask. She is gone now and leaving the vet's clinic, I desperately needed someone to hold me, to embrace me, sympathize, and cry with me. But in these times, I couldn't drive to my closest friends and ask for this. I can't even imagine what this scenario must be for those who have lost family members.

Now, finally, the earth has begun to warm even in this northern location where March and April are sometimes brutal ends of winter. As I am able to go outside now, conversing with neighbors or friends while maintaining distance, the memories of those long, lonely hours of everyday from mid-March to now are beginning to fade. Questions however remain: Can we go back to what life was like before COVID-19? Are there positive things that might come out of this global disaster? Will we still be fearful and wary around others? How can our communities of choice come together again? What will that look like? Scarier, will we go into the winter with re-occurrences of the virus that will force us back into isolation? I ask myself: How can I live through another winter of aloneness? What can I do to prepare myself for that possibility? Each of us have so many questions.

We're Going to Be Alright
by Faye Boom

Born in 1941 in Oconto Falls, Wisconsin,
Faye Boom is a retired Attorney and
lives in Bozeman, Montana.

Our reality today, because of the COVID-19 virus, is different than anything we ever expected. No longer can we hug our family and friends. When out in public, we have become wary of any person around us. Are they carrying the dreaded virus? Are they wearing a mask? We don't want to get too close. Will we ever be the same when this is over or will we have become inured to isolation, and timid in our interactions? Will we be able to come out of this experience with the same vigor as when we were deposited into it?

Growing up on a small dairy farm in Wisconsin in the 40s and 50s, I learned to make do with what we had at home rather than running into town. That, coupled with what my family calls "Midwestern frugality," has equipped me, to some extent, to live in this desperate "stay-at-home" culture we are now in. In cooking and baking on the farm, we made things from what we had in the cupboard rather than run out for something else. Did you know you could make baking powder or sweetened condensed milk at home? If I need a piece of material that I don't have, I will look through my closets or drawers to find a usable and disposable piece of clothing that I can cut up. Old curtains? Just like in *The Sound of Music*, they have many uses. If I don't have toothpaste, I will mix up salt and baking soda. I can make do.

I fear many young people haven't learned the coping skills of past generations. Most of them have not lived in really hard times. They have grown up in an economy of disposable products and electronic devices; even the electronic devices are disposable. They have learned that if they run out of something they can always go to the store and buy more. They can replace an outdated or impaired device rather than fix it. We, the older generation, trying so hard to please them, have not taught them how to survive hard times. They will be more frustrated than their elders at having to do without, having to stay home, having to seclude themselves.

As to the poorer people among us, to some extent they are also equipped to make do. What is different for them is they have never known plenty and have little to fall back on if they need to sequester themselves. They may not have music, smart phones, email, or books to entertain themselves. They may not have the means to get to a store to get necessities. They may not have a network of "helpers." It may be up to the rest of us to seek them out and help them cope.

Women and children in families that are ordered to stay home are further threatened by the exception of take-out alcohol to the rules about closed businesses. The combination of worries about money if the wage earner's job is lost, enforced close proximity, unfilled time, and abundant alcohol leads to a hostile environment ripe for abuse, and that is not just in the poorer families. The victims of this abuse are going to have a harder time reaching out for help because now they are confined on the same premises as the abuser.

Also, I think of our poor, polluted earth. It must be taking a breath of fresh air during this downturn in human activity. Very few airplanes are flying and leaving vapors in their wake. The roads are quiet, many fewer exhaust fumes in the air. The cruise lines are stilled and not adding their pollution to the oceans. And among my friends, people are in their backyards cleaning up and getting their gardens and lawns ready for spring without adding the chemicals that inhibit the lives of the worms and insects so necessary to proper growth. Maybe we will learn that all of it is not as necessary as we thought. Maybe we can be still, and cherish and preserve the earth.

The stay-at-home orders affect my social life and activist life, but

I will be okay. I enjoy being home and I have learned to entertain myself. I am reminded to be grateful for a warm home, enough food, and family and friends that look out for me. When it is over, hopefully, I will embrace my friends and joyously go to meetings, lectures, yes, and maybe even a movie. But if, by some chance, I contract the deadly disease, what are my fears? I don't mind dying. I have lived a long and good life. On the other hand , it is said to be a horrible death. I could dwell on that and fret about what it would be like but I choose not to. I will be careful but I will operate on the assumption that all will be fine.

What I would say to my young friends is this: Be happy with yourself, the one person you have to live with forever. Make good friends and work at keeping your relationships alive. Live within your means. Be careful of what debt you incur. You never know what is going to happen. Whatever it is, above all, know you are not alone! When you need help, ask for it. Be open to learning whatever lessons you can learn from this time. We will come out of his period of hardship and tribulation. And when it is over, don't forget those lessons. Perhaps we will realize that it is not the dollar economy that is all-important; it is the people, the citizens not only of our family and neighborhood, or of this country, but around the globe.

Hoping on Hope
by Dorothy Bradley

Born in 1947 in Madison, Wisconsin,
Dorothy Bradley is a retired Attorney, Activist,
and former Montana Legislator
and lives in Clyde Park, Montana.

I was named after my grandmother and I used to wish my name was something else. Today, I find it astonishing that I took the time to reflect on something as small as whether I liked my grandmother's name. Today, the important thing about my grandparents is that I am among the fortunate to have known all four of them. I think about them, and I am aware of the sense of rootedness and stability they imparted, which helps keep me tethered in this boundless universe and beleaguered world.

This spring of 2020, I am accommodating the COVID-19 challenge with an eerie sense of inevitability. On one hand, my retirement lifestyle at age 73 is relatively unchanged. I have the stunning luxury of a daily run on a high bench road when I am intensely loving the seasons, the waving passersby, the slow moving tractor, the fussing ravens, the squalls, the wind in the spruce, my level of energy. I look down at green pastures speckled with grazing cows, and marvel that this was part of Plenty Coups' vision in the flanking Crazy Mountains some 160 years ago. This, too, keeps me grounded.

But a new wrinkle in my outlook is my shortening fuse with the human species. Why aren't we prepared to meet this challenge head on?

I grew up with a scientist father. Table topics included the possibility—the inevitability—of a pandemic, over-population, water shortages, super bugs, species extinctions. Because I trusted my father, I have always trusted science and scientists. At age 22, I decided against bringing children into this world after studying the predictions of overpopulation. And I have always accepted the likelihood that I would experience some kind of great human suffering in my lifetime: mass migration, starvation, plague, whatever. But actually embracing this present global catastrophe is beyond my mortal capability. I find myself glued to the news as if it is a movie thriller. Every now and then I force myself into crunches and stretches in front of MSNBC thinking I should do something constructive while I listen to this unfolding drama. My face gets tired and I realize it is so scrunched up with agitation that my muscles are aching.

For some reason I assumed that our educated reaction to this pandemic would immediately transfer into our seriously addressing the pending climate crisis. We would collectively say, "Oh, now we get it!" No sign of that. I visit our local garbage dump and stare in disbelief that my neighbors can't take a minute to flatten recyclable cardboard. I conjure up images of the billions of plastic gloves and masks washing onto the island of plastic in the mid-Pacific. When I help stock our local grocery store, I am aghast that people eat thrice packaged frozen waffles when they could, in this time of food shortages, buy a bag of Krusteaz Waffle Mix, or even, flour. And in this spring season, I smell chemicals in the air and know little thought is given to the pollinators.

My lifelong commitment is to leave this planet a better place—my home, my valley, my state, my country. And we, the most environmentally literate of all civilizations, are leaving it in peril.

Will this virus crisis pass in my life time, or will it linger? Or will it evolve into something worse? Or might it help us become better, kinder, smarter? I don't know. Where is our visionary Plenty Coups showing us an aspiration—a path?

As I rest in the shadow of the Crazies, I will focus on the one thing we can all always do that will never be at risk: spreading the love. Because love absolutely and unquestionably is our most sacred and inviolable gift; and second, I must continue my crusade on behalf of the planet, because it truly is in peril and it is the ever smoldering fire in my belly.

My father observed, "I separate my hopes from my expectations.
I have expectations. But I always have hope."

"Hope" is the thing with feathers—
That perches in the soul—
And sings the tunes without the words—
And never stops—at all—

And sweetest—in the Gale—is heard—
And sore must be the storm—
That could abash the little Bird
that kept so many warm—

I've heard it in the chillest land—
And on the strangest Sea—
Yet—never—in Extremity, It asked a crumb—of me.

—Emily Dickinson, "'Hope' is the Thing with Feathers," 1861

These Corona Days
by Collette Brooks-Hops

Born in 1946 in Los Angeles, California,
Collette Brooks-Hops is an artist
and lives in Bozeman, Montana.

I am on the other side of looking forward: old by some standards but still young in my own mind. In these Corona Days, I find myself thinking of the past while groping for a future. Along with concern for my autistic son, faraway children, and the daunting task of grocery shopping, I'm learning to be clear and organized, keeping errands to a minimum. Zoom adds another layer of distance to my already deep sense of loss. My husband is seriously ill. Our laughter is brave. We hug each other and chat like tomorrow is coming.

My mom used to say to me, "Some things are worth a good cry!"

My Italian dad, an artist/painter/sign writer, worked at Paramount Studios and never quit trying to figure out how things worked. My German mom baked bread and raised six of us to clean up after ourselves. Both avid readers, they honored curiosity and allowed each of us our own voice.

My own long journey of dreaming, working, teaching art, exhibiting, deep breathing, raising kids, praying, traveling, collecting, recycling, furniture finishing, painting, murals, signwriting, stage scenery, and pondering, has brought me to this moment, wondering what an artist is supposed to be. I still don't know.

Calling myself "artist" has never felt comfortable. I see things. I feel things. Sometimes, I try to interpret what I see with paint, dirt, and stuff I put together to hear the story it has to tell. Connecting with people, things and ideas compels me, and I try to do a bit of that everyday. The master's program was helpful but making art has always been my best teacher. Art is my form of activism. Art is what's happening right where I am, like this thing called Corona, which is anything but a garland, wreath or crown.

"I am fairly certain that given a proper cape and corona, I could save the world!" I have that sign posted in my kitchen.

Webster's definitions of words are deceiving, but an image has a way of thrusting truth forward, a sort of shortcut to understanding. Put them together and you have an icon to read. Logos et Imago. I look to Montana's starry sky to help me experience some stardust within. It's always just out of my reach, close as a quiet moment.

My concentration is easily lost and many unfinished works stare at me from dusty corners in my studio. It's more fun to bring others together to encounter creatively than to resolve a struggling art piece. Pondering and wandering through my workspace, my heart is trying, unconvincingly, to stay present to what is in front of me. I cannot speak to those who are not able to stay at home and have to be on the front line everyday, those who have young children or live with abusive spouses. My challenge is to care for my husband, my special needs son, stay present to my children, chop veggies and carry water for the piles of dishes that show up every day and do it all with some semblance of normalcy during this non-normal time. "Follow the rules and stay put!" blast the newscasters. Walks with my dog and grocery hunting and gathering help me to see how very precious life is and to find everyday ways to celebrate that knowing. For me, that's the daily challenge of Corona.

I painted a funny face on a mask, and my husband brought gales of laughter to the nurses who drew his blood. I will paint prayer banners for the front of our home, give away art supplies to neighbors with little ones and try to do what little things I can in my own Corona of influence.

Everyday, I am grateful to be on this side of the grass, Thank you to Corona for slowing me down in some ways, but I must say, the novelty of this "novel" Corona virus is wearing thin!

Mixed Media: acrylic and gold leaf

This is My Body

by Collette Brooks-Hops

This is My Body
It is time, Now.
To quit the burnt offerings
of Earth's provisions.
False narratives that unravel life to its simplest form
Truths and untruths keep us
confused, isolated, at odds.
Some are leaving, Oh Merciful Breath!
Some will remain, in angst and insomnia.
Crying out
To take heed
To evolve
To work
To love
To stand in the Daylight
Singing, singing . . .
Singing our bones
Back to the living.
Some will see beyond this Time
Moving toward, not away.
Holding the tension.
Betwixt Life and Death.
No Hands of an Unseen god to rescue me.
This is My Body.

Meditation on Place
by Glen Chamberlain

Born in 1950 in Delphi, Indiana,
Glen Chamberlain, author/writer, is a retired
English Professor at Montana State University
and resides in Bozeman, Montana.

Over the past weeks, I have heard friends describe their situations: they are isolated, locked down, quarantined, sheltering in place. The various descriptions reminded me of a conversation Hamlet has with Rosencrantz about being in Denmark. Rosencrantz doesn't mind at all, while Hamlet does, and these opposing perceptions cause Hamlet to muse, ". . . for there is nothing either good or bad, but thinking makes it so." And thinking—at least for humans—requires words, and while some of these words connote negativity, others don't. This is why, over the past weeks, I have decided to view myself as merely being-in-place.

And what does being-in-place mean? A place is a portion of space, a portion one is in or one is not. As I write this, my portion is a chair at my dining table. When I pause, I look out to my backyard, where there are four mature aspen trees whose buds are just unfurling into fluorescence, a mountain ash whose small fists of green push tentatively against the brown leaves that died in place with last September's early winter, and a tamarack (so out of place on this side of the Divide) needling the air around it. Dandelions proliferate, and as much as their profligacy frustrates me, we don't spray them, because soon the pine siskins, so delicate that they can light on the stems and pluck the flowers, will be here; and the poison will harm the worms living under the weeds, the worms that bring the robins who pull and rip them from their places.

Besides the robins, this spring, for the first time, two crows—I suppose a male and female—have come to our backyard. They feast on the suet and cautiously accept the nuts and bread my husband presents them. Their place is somewhere else, but they spend a good portion of the day here, and they often scare and sometimes chase many of the other birds off. They make me wonder who has the right to the backyard, whose place it should be, and I think of those old lyrics: "'Tis a gift to be simple, 'tis a gift to be free," and I stumble over the next line: is it a gift to come down where we want or where we ought to be, because the former is full of intention, and the latter of fate. And that question brings me back to my place in this world, this house situated on the northern edge of Bozeman, Montana, where I can look beyond my backyard to the subdivision that just seven years ago was field. It was then that people who wanted to live here filled it. I can't be critical of them, as I am here because I wanted to be, and perhaps it is the want that creates the ought.

Beyond their rooftops stand the Bridger Mountains. When, as was the case for Wordsworth, this world is too much with me, getting and spending till my powers have been wasted, I hike the drainages, and, eventually, like a pine siskin, I light on a place where I ought to be. For then.

For now, I am in place, in a chair at my dining table. I am not isolated, locked down, quarantined, or even sheltering. I am merely here. There is plenty to do, if I am disciplined. I think of the story of Ikkyu Sojun, a Zen master, who once was approached by a man who asked him to please write a maxim of the highest wisdom he had gained from years of meditating in one place. Ikkyu took his brush and wrote "Attention." "Is that all?" asked the man. Ikkyu then wrote, "Attention, Attention."

I'm So Tired . . .
by Jessie Close

Born in 1953 in Greenwich, Connecticut,
Jessie Close is a writer, photographer, and artist
and lives in Bozeman, Montana.

I'm on my bed. Again. Taking a break from writing. I've spent many hours in my bedroom lately because of COVID-19. I don't actually get under the covers, but lie on the quilt and against my pillows to read. Much neater that way. My three little dogs, Snitz, Goodness, and Gracious, always come up on the bed with me. They're comforting and not judgmental in the least: a superior kind of thinking. My bedroom is lit by four windows that face the street—bay windows without the bay; the light changes with the hour and weather. Goodness and Gracious enjoy sitting on the back of the little couch beneath the windows. They bark when dogs with people walk by, but surprisingly don't bark when people without dogs walk by. Interesting.

Within the small circle of loved ones I interact with, this scourge is just called 'COVID'. We needn't say the 19 every time. I'm tired of that word: COVID. It stinks of death and upheaval, and you-know-who: Trump.

I'm grateful to work at home; my studio is upstairs. I'm writing a novel that transports me to another time, a time when I was young in the 50s and 60s. I'm now one month shy of 67.

My sisters are 73 and 75 years old and it's for them, and myself, that I'm being so careful. And for my three grandchildren, ages one, three and six. In the beginning the scientists and doctors believed that children were not affected by this coronavirus disease. They have since changed their minds and know that children can and do get sick: very very sick. My heart! I couldn't bear it if one of my grand babies succumbed to COVID-19.

I wear a mask and gloves every time I go out, keep a bottle of disinfectant in my purse to spray on the gloves before I take them off.

I think of the families of the dead. They are many more in number than the dead. So I stay in my house. I'm not particularly unhappy about that, it's a simple and effective way to make sure my family doesn't have to mourn me.

I have become excessively aware of my mental illness during this time; I live with manic-depression, also referred to as Bipolar Disorder Type 1. Throughout these months of isolation, the ups and downs have become annoying. I appreciate the ups, if I don't actually become manic. I do not appreciate the downs although I haven't approached anything like suicide; that's in the past. When I need to pick up my medications, I don my mask and gloves. I have five medications that keep me on the straight and narrow most of the time. And I have a schedule that helps. But during this time of COVID-19 my medications haven't completely stilled my mood disorder.

I was forced to isolate away from my sisters and grandchildren for two weeks in March because of a possible COVID exposure. In the beginning I was excited to be in the position to write uninterrupted. I was uninterrupted, but couldn't write. I felt loneliness, an emotion I never feel under usual circumstances, where two weeks felt like two months. I had groceries delivered. I was on the phone more than usual. At the two week mark I busted out of my house; I still wouldn't hug my sisters. And because of my sisters, my grandchildren were off limits, too, in case they were carrying COVID-19.

I watch the news every weekday evening for just an hour; that's all I can tolerate. I see how many people have died of COVID that day, what the cumulative number is and how many doctors and nurses are working tirelessly, and how many of them have died. I feel as though we are stuck in a bad Twilight Zone episode, or possibly a Hitchcock film. I feel helpless. I grieve. And I get angry. So so so angry! I try to keep my temper in check, but have found great relief by getting on my phone or computer and writing to the White House. It's easy. Try it. One of my sisters told me to be careful, that I was going to get into trouble, but I continue. Words are nothing compared to what he has done: no COVID tests!! No tests until it was too late for thousands of souls. And he'll never see my words. If he did he'd discard them when he learns that I'm not a billionaire.

I have heard friends say they'll move to another country if The Orange (the color of CAUTION! STAY AWAY!) is re-elected. I have faith in us, our people, the American people, and I don't think he has a chance in hell. If he's re-elected it will be because he manipulated the votes, or because Putin helped his lapdog. We the People didn't elect Orange in the first place. Three million votes were discounted because of the Electoral College. The popular vote is not respected, yet. I digress. But I won't leave my country.

This coronavirus is simply that: a virus. The virus itself isn't political, it doesn't consciously choose who it lands on and infects, it's not a Democrat or Republican or a Green Party or an Independent virus.

If you happen to be without a mask, COVID-19 finds your mouth, the easiest entry into your body. I get angry when I see the percentage of people who don't bother protecting themselves. They put us all at risk, and for WHAT? I suspect many of them are Republicans or they just don't care if they spread the coronavirus disease. Or they're really stupid. And why are politics involved? And why is the Orange Buffoon pushing for religious people to gather? I guarantee he doesn't love God, in any form. He knows Christians will vote for him, (something I really don't 'get'), and he has no moral fiber; he's putting them in danger and he knows it. He doesn't care because he is a narcissist, a psychopath, and ugly on top of all that. I wish Melania would walk out on him.

If I can't hug my grandchildren soon I'll implode. I miss them so much! When feelings of loss and anxiety hit me, I retreat to my beautiful bedroom where Goodness, Gracious, and Snitz add to the calm. I am anxious, as we all are, for this COVID-19 to leave us; I hope and pray that all this death stops soon.

Germy Creatures that I Will and Will Not Miss
by Susie Cole

Born in 1943 in Hamilton, Montana,
Susie Cole is a retired Water Authority Director
for San Diego County and lives in Sun City, Arizona.

Life during a pandemic was not anything I ever imagined. At 76, I do remember the days before the polio vaccine was developed. Our parents were fearful. We kids were reminded to be careful. My late husband, George, contracted polio at age five and spent several weeks in the hospital—some of the time in an iron lung. He was fortunate to pretty much fully recover after many months of physical therapy. He did remember the time when all the neighbors and friends were afraid to be around his family.

The here and now of the COVID-19 outbreak is much more real to me than the childhood fear of polio. I have lived alone for over five years, so the isolation has not been an issue. From the beginning, I made the conscientious decision that I needed a broader definition of family than just those who live with me. To me, it has included those who I see on a very regular basis. Thus, I've visited, dined, hiked, and kayaked with my brother, sister-in-law, and a few friends. I know where they have been and how healthy they are. I have been taking the social distancing seriously, but I still do my own grocery shopping and errand running. When I'm around the general public, I wear my face mask and, sometimes gloves. To this point, almost one month in, the shutdown hasn't been too hard to endure. Time will tell whether I feel this same way six months from now.

I do miss many of the activities I was involved in before the shutdown. I like being around people. I live in a 55 Plus Community in the Phoenix area that has multiple recreation centers with lots of activities. All of that is shut down now except for golf, which is being run under safe social distancing rules. Looking to the future, since our community demographics are mostly people in the vulnerable category, it is hard to imagine they will open our recreation centers at the same time as ones that cater to the general public. This will be felt even more during the very hot weather when traditionally most outdoor activities cease. Another of my activities that has been canceled is tutoring first and second graders. Will this be available anytime soon? Will it be wise to go among those little germy creatures? I will really miss it if I have to give it up for good.

As I age, I know that my ability to do various activities will diminish. Has this pandemic hastened that process? I've always had alternative activities in the back of my mind to take the place of the more physical ones I can still do. When will I say now is the time I really dig into genealogy? One thing that has been confirmed during this time—I really, truly, do not like housecleaning. Cooking? I'm all for it, but that darn dust just keeps coming back. And travel? Was Indonesia my last international trip?

My preferred at-home activities reflect my mathematical, logical background. I love jigsaw puzzles, sudoku puzzles, *The New York Times* crosswords and my subscription to *Math and Logic Puzzles* that I've had for several years. I do love reading both fiction and non-fiction. I've expanded to regularly downloading audiobooks and eBooks from the library. Multi-tasking now means listening to an audiobook while working on a jigsaw puzzle. I have not become an artist, poet, seamstress, crafter, or any of those things I thought I might do. So, this is me. The same old me. Good, old, logical Susie.

So, what about the future? I've told my kids I do not want to be put on a ventilator. I will be careful and not take too many chances. But, it very well could be COVID-19 that kills me. Does that scare me? Not necessarily. I've lived a good life and done many things. As a retiree with good pensions and savings, I don't have the worries and uncertainties of someone younger. I tend not to be a worrier and don't plan to start now.

Thoughts Brought to Light with COVID-19
by Mary E. Costello

Born in 1941 in Great Falls, Montana,
Mary Costello is a retired nurse actively managing
a ranch and resides in Stevensville, Montana.

When Dr. Fauci spoke in Hamilton, Montana last year on a visit to the Rocky Mountain Lab (operated by the National Institute of Allergy and Infectious Diseases), he said he had worked with seven different presidential administrations on infectious diseases. He said something was coming and it could be a pandemic.

Now we are in the midst of the Covid-19 pandemic and it includes social distancing and isolating ourselves in place.

I am 78 years old, a retired registered nurse with a BSN from Montana State College (now Montana State University), and an active farmer-rancher. I have spent most of life living on a ranch. In my working career I worked in hospitals and in public health. The majority of my patients were underserved and unentitled people.

I have been a widow for eleven years. As a farm woman and a widow, I have spent many years alone. In some ways this time feels the same. Being alone is sometimes stressful, as is the knowledge that it will continue.

It concerns me that so many people are already homeless and now more families will become homeless. Children are hungry. I have never been hungry. Lives are shattered. There are many who care and do what they can to help. There are others, young and old, who don' t care enough to do anything.

If I were in a city apartment, I would feel claustrophobic, but here I have acres to walk and ride in. I can garden, hang out clothes to dry in the sunshine, walk outside, go look at the baby calves, see the sky.

I would say to us and to future generations: If you want a future, get going. No one will do it for you. Accumulate less, consume less, recycle more, look out for others, be generous with your time and give as much as you can. Learn to be thankful for what you have and to accept responsibility for your actions and your own happiness.

Silent Spring
by Betsy Danforth

Born in 1961 in New Jersey, Betsy Danforth
is the Director of Montana State University
Women's Center and lives in Bozeman, Montana.

Graduation for Montana State University was Saturday, May 9th. Where the hell is the class of 2020? Main street . . . downtown . . . no one to be seen. The bars reported 10-20 patrons on graduation night! Talk about Silent Spring. The town's dead.

Speaking of . . . in two and a half months, COVID-19 has left 90,000 Americans dead. Our President doesn't give a damn, not a glimmer of caring, not the tiniest peek into what should be a soul. Just a gaping black hole of narcissism and poison. But I digress; it's easy to do these days if you read two sentences of any news story. Really, an article's title usually does it.

Wear your face mask.

Wash-your-hands-for-twenty-seconds-singing-Happy-Birthday-two-times-in-a-row.

This morning I woke to a headline (I know. I try not to look at my phone first thing in the morning, but there it was): *Why Some Nurses Have Decided to Leave Their Profession*. Are you kidding me? I can't believe any of them are still practicing, especially without personal protective equipment (PPE). Sure . . . now bandanas are acceptable replacements for N95 masks. Why can't you be tough like us politicians, talking heads, so-called leaders? Hey, you don't need all that ridiculous PPE.

People are actually criticizing nurses for leaving the profession, nurses who have given decades of their lives to help, care for, comfort, and cure others.

What were you doing that whole time Trump, Pence, Redfield, Azar, and Hahn? Oh, that's right, you were the guys up on podiums reassuring everyone that this was containable, not a problem, that "the risk at this time is low." After the first reported American death on February 29th (how many others have there been?), the CDC Director, Dr. Robert Redfield said, "The American public needs to go on with their normal lives." This is the expert, THE guy. This is the Director of the CDC!

Of course it's not just about the United States, despite what Donald Trump thinks. Worldwide, there are currently 284,674 deaths, and 4,215,317 cases. Most real experts agree that the virus is just getting started.

Just. Getting. Started.

And, we haven't seen the worst of it yet. Some experts say, not by a long shot.

Wear your face mask, use your hand sanitizer.

Some of us Americans are privileged beyond belief, including me. We have accessible food, homes to be sequestered in, televisions, computers, Netflix, books to read, music to listen to, soap and clean water with which to wash-our-hands-for-twenty-seconds-singing-Happy-Birthday-two-times-in-a-row.

But, there can be no denying that the poor and elderly are dying at much more rapid rates. Folks in assisted living facilities and nursing homes are basically imprisoned in what have become death traps. People like to say that this virus is the great equalizer. Not true. Take New York City, for instance, the farther one gets away from downtown Manhattan, the more likely one is to die. I'm betting coronavirus disease deaths can be directly correlated to income levels. I'm also betting the darker your skin is, the more likely you are to die. Trump's dream—could he have imagined it? The brown and black people dropping like flies, and he didn't even have to kill them!

Oh, but he did kill them with his epic incompetence, his denial, and by not acting urgently and decisively, by treating this as a public relations crisis, instead of a public health crisis, by inciting protests against stay-at-home policies, by saying things like "what have we got to lose?" Far too many times, by insisting states open back up far too early to stimulate the economy. Pressuring the meatpacking industry to get those factories up and running, though many factories have seen more than 50% of their workers fall ill with COVID-19. And let's not forget Trump asking about drinking-Clorox-as-a-cure.

Wash your hands. Wear your face mask.

Has this been the longest of Springs or does it just seem that way because of our "new normal"? One wonderful thing my partner and I have really seen, probably for the first time, is this transition to spring. The buds on the trees outside our windows get bigger every day, their slow transition to leaves, every little crocus, every daffodil popping up through the earth. This is no small thing, to observe, to notice, to be aware of a season's transition.

Mostly, I feel ridiculously removed from the whole nightmare that is COVID-19 for many people. I have a job that I get to do remotely. I have not had anyone in my life fall seriously ill or die. I have zoom dates and distance drinks with friends. I am personally so grateful, at least fifty times every day, that I have a yard, space, and vast nature surrounding me. Most of my friends are baking bread, working from home, spending unprecedented amounts of time with their kids, making masks to donate to healthcare workers, and donating blood. I think about those being forced because of basic economics to go to a job that ensures their exposure to the virus. Or being a senior in a nursing home who cannot see or hug their family. Or being stuck in a prison cell with a coughing cellmate. Or being trapped in a home with a violent and abusive partner. It is unimaginable.

There can be no doubt that our world has changed forever. My dreams tend to focus on whether people are wearing their masks or if there are too many of us in a room. I see parties or restaurants full of people on television programs and realize it now makes me anxious. I continue to wonder—daydream—what our country's situation would be if we had a real leader, a brave and soulful president with foresight, who listened to the advice of science, experts, professionals. Someone kind of like that last guy.

The silver linings? We have seen instances of people working together to help those in peril and individuals whose actions border on the heroic. The little girl who took her pony to the window of a nursing home to cheer up the residents, the various businesses offering free food, the Kansas farmer who sent (#inlovewithcuomo) Governor Cuomo one of the five masks he had left with a heartfelt letter. I like to think this is who we are, this is the United States of America. Maybe this surreal dark period in human history will help us all learn to live more simply? Maybe more people will listen to science and logic? *Maybe* we will get a new administration. Please, goddess, let the American people elect a new president!

Something Evolving as History Repeats
by Jean Davis

Born in 1920 in Ohio, Jean Davis
lives in Helena, Montana.

Plans for my 100th birthday party on Easter this year were turned upside down with the arrival of the COVID-19 pandemic, but family and staff found other ways to celebrate and the day turned out to be quite memorable. Living in a retirement community, my days are spent in my apartment. Meals are delivered. My temperature and heart rate are checked daily. My apartment has a beautiful view out across the Helena Valley where I can see city activity, watch the weather, and see snow-capped mountains. News watching is kept to a minimum. My computer or iPad afford access to the world, and provide books, entertainment and family contact.

My life began as the Spanish flu epidemic was winding down. My early childhood years were spent during the Great Depression followed by World War II. All of these events impacted my life in different ways, but none so personally as this epidemic, ordering parts of my daily life that I cannot control.

Looking back, my life has been a good one. My childhood was a happy one with loving parents and two older brothers. We lived in a middle class urban neighborhood in northern Ohio. There are fond memories of neighborhood fun. School was an important and enjoyable part of my life. All of these times leave pleasant memories to reflect upon.

A wartime romance and wedding bells brought me to Montana,

gave me three wonderful daughters (each now married), two grandsons, and a granddaughter. None live close, but all keep in touch by email, phone, and now virtual visiting.

Although I have lived alone for the past sixteen years, the current situation is quite different. As of this writing, I am in my fifth week of "stay-in-place" orders, but do not feel stressed.

Keeping a more or less regular schedule is helpful. Being able to take care of myself and handle my own business affairs keeps me feeling somewhat in charge. Basic good health is a plus.

The enormity of the death toll brought on by the pandemic is hard for me to fathom. To see endless coffins side by side and to know that each one represents a loved one lost is heartbreaking beyond belief.

The stay-in-place order creates unimaginable hardships for many as they face unemployment, loss of wages, children at home trying to keep up with their school work, and little ones underfoot to be kept busy. Other families continue to face poverty and abusive situations. Those who can must reach out to these families and give them support in whatever way they can. As things improve they should not be forgotten.

Whenever things return to *normal* living, perhaps we should rethink what is normal. Do we rush out to go to a restaurant, a movie, a football game or some other entertainment? Of course we will. But we should still stay close as families, enjoy times together, visit friends and extended family, and get better acquainted with our neighbors. We need to rethink what is important in our lives.

When this current situation slows and things begin to return to our "new normal" my life will see some pleasant changes. Meals will be enjoyed with fellow residents, card games, and other activities will resume. And best of all, my family will be able to visit me.

The unthinkable loss of life and the turning upside down of many lives should remind us to be ever vigilant. We must be prepared to meet and overcome whatever the future brings.

Pandemic 2020—A Global Wake Up Call
by Mallery Downs

Born in 1953 in Fond du Lac, Wisconsin,
Mallery Downs is a Program Manager and Registered Nurse
and lives in Albuquerque, New Mexico.

I have procrastinated writing this and I am glad I did. As time goes by my feelings have changed and I am even more concerned than I was a month ago. I worry now about how and when people will be able to go back to work and school. I worry that people are desperate and will not continue to practice social distancing and wearing masks. I worry that there will be even more people infected and more will die because of lack of national leadership.

During my career as a registered nurse, I worked in environmental public health and learned a lot about how our environment and health are impacted by the human influence on the earth. It is so interesting that during the pandemic the canals in Venice have cleared, birds in Central Park are singing more since they are less stressed by the noise of traffic, and air quality has improved around the world. I keep hoping we will learn how much damage we are doing to the earth when we get back to even a 'new normal'. I think about the impact humans have had on the earth and how we have abused it through population growth, extractive industries, and pollution. I believe the earth is sending the message, with a pandemic, that if we don't stop the abuse then it shall take care of itself by reducing the human population. It appears that the Coronavirus disease might be one of the solutions. I hope we pay attention to this global wake-up call.

I cut out a cartoon from the July 2007 *Albuquerque Journal* that I thought was perfect and hung it above my work desk until retirement. Set in a medical exam room, Earth, the patient, is on the exam table, and the doctor reads from his chart to the Earth, "The bad news is you've got advanced-stage humans. The good news is they've just about run their course and you should be on the mend soon."

I feel very fortunate to live in New Mexico and have a governor and mayor who have been proactive in all the public health measures and who will not re-open until the infection rates continue to go down. We are still encouraged to stay home and everyone is required to wear a mask. I hate seeing people out and about who aren't wearing masks and would love to have a catchy come back, but have been warned by friends that this could result in a serious confrontation (the media reported that someone got shot after confronting someone). We are fortunate to have next door neighbors whom we visit with on a regular basis and are part of our family unit. We still visit outdoors and keep some distance, but it has definitely helped us feel less isolated.

I know I have been fortunate in my circumstances and have not felt deprived staying home. I must admit that there has been little that has been stressful about this 'in place' time. Since retirement our days have been much less stressful as they are now. Some of the small stresses for us include some disappointment that we can't take long car trips and visit friends, but since I can't sit for long periods right now due to having sacroiliac (S I) joint pain, it's easy to accept staying home.

Shopping is a bit more stressful since picking up groceries curb side is always an unknown, and they often don't have what I ordered days ago. We need a curtain rod and clear trash bags. I ordered online three days ago and I am still waiting for a message to pick up the order. We wanted a dog and tried to adopt, but had a terrible experience, and we can't try again because the shelter's adoption program is closed. So, I am learning patience. Although, I haven't succeeded yet, I am getting better.

My husband Bert has short-term memory problems, but has finally recognized that we are staying-in-place, wearing masks, and is finally accepting this is the new routine. I also realize what small inconveniences these situations are, especially compared to what I see on television.

We worry about our son since his job has been impacted, but fortunately his employer got a loan from the Feds. His wife is a teacher who has continued her salary and works from home. I only hope that others less fortunate have been able to find some support.

I see some of the efforts people are doing in the news and think to myself: why aren't we doing all these helpful efforts all the time? In Albuquerque, the homeless have more shelters, opportunities for food, and medical care than ever—why not all the time?! We can make the same point for all the issues getting attention now.

As things open up I will continue to keep social distancing and wearing a mask. I find that no matter what, masks are not all that comfortable and I get rather hot and cranky at times. I hope that once a vaccine is out, we can do away with the masks. Ever since I took microbiology in college, I have been cautious about touching surfaces, and rarely open a public door with my hands.

If I were to give any advice to future generations it would be to please take better care of the earth than all the previous generations have. I fear it may be too little, too late.

What If This Were The Time?
by Teresa Durrant

Born in 1949 in Salt Lake City, Utah, Teresa Durrant
is a former Nurse and retired Biomedical Research Trainer
and lives in Cuenca, Ecuador.

What if this were *the time*? If this were *the end*? It's possible. Mother Earth strikes back. Reclaims her own. And the deer and the dolphin return. And the sky is blue again. And the air is fresh and feels good in your chest. The pathways are thick with bright yellow dandelions. And all you can hear is the river.

I don't begrudge the Earth. We've been poor caretakers. We've been users, takers, profiteers. Not all of us, but enough of us, so that what we have to hand our children is our unending collective trash that covers this spectacular blue orb from stem to stern. Our people are divided. Children are held in cages. And the disparity of income and resources in our world is inexcusable. Power does corrupt. Greed is not a virtue.

But that world is different from my personal experience here, high in the Andes. I literally am surrounded by beauty. El Rio Tomebamba is right out the door. I have enough here to entertain myself for a decade. My friends and family are safe. Food is delivered, trash is picked up three times a week. Our water is pure, right out of the tap. And my friends do yoga three times a week on Zoom. The lovely solitude is broken up by the errands that even now, we have to do. I revel in these simple acts. People, all masked, still greet each other, still smile when eyes meet. And on the street is the best place to give to those asking for money to buy food for their, mostly, Venezuelan families. Giving a little bit here means a lot. The expat community in Cuenca gives generously to causes and volunteers for projects that benefit the poor and disadvantaged, taking food up into the mountains even now.

So, the only stressful thing for me during this pandemic is to find a way to integrate those two views of reality. My personal life is happy. My view of the rest of the world, bleak. I do take credit for the happy part, but the rest of it falls on all of us, too. Is consciously living enough? My generation was inspired. We thought we would change the world. But did we? Not enough. We have awesome new inventions, but massive numbers of our people are going to bed hungry. We have spectacular machines that can do anything we can ask, but children are being stolen and passed around for sex.

So Mother Earth has given us a wake up call. We have a choice: we can do nothing, or we can commit to doing more in whatever way meets our circumstances. Being an activist is one of the things I am grateful to have experienced in my relatively long life. I learned in nursing school that I am more powerful as an advocate for someone else than I ever could be for myself. And we also need to balance what we do with who we are in the place we find ourselves. For instance, I have enough. I've been enough places and seen enough things and the pleasure I get from those memories sustains me when I can't leave the house. I've had good luck and been loved and know without a doubt that I am in a better situation than most of the world's people. I have always known that our connections are more important than our things. Standing up for what is right, is still the answer. Love is more powerful than fear. Compassion is us at our best. But we must speak louder for those that are bearing more than their share. This world is over-rich. We need a more even playing field. We can't sustain a generation of young people with crippling debt, trying to start a life and family. Every child deserves enough food to eat and education and shelter. Every person with demons in their heads deserves treatment. Every woman in the world deserves a safe place to live. Basic human rights. I guess that's what I still commit to fighting for. Whether it's showing respect to the man asking for money, or making eye contact with someone in pain or grief, or giving generously to organizations that support those in need. I remind myself that time is not always linear. The good we do, the love and respect we give, the compassion we feel and show goes out beyond our physical sphere. We will never know the impact, but I do know that the kindness of strangers will take me to my knees, time after time. We have to do better for people. For our children. For our families. For each other.

And I would tell anyone coming along after me, you are the person who decides the kind of person you become. Consciously or unconsciously, you are molding yourself. If you admire kindness, be kind. If you admire integrity, practice it. If you respect hard work, work hard.

Don't send the universe mixed messages. Get in the habit of knowing your intention in any given situation. Then, if a question of doing one thing or another comes up, check in with your intentions. You don't always have to do the thing you know is the best, but you do have to make that decision consciously if you want personal growth.

We are one. We are our sister's keeper. Our brother's keeper. Be kind. You do not know what pain another carries. Don't add to it.

You are more awesome than you know.

A Letter from My Great-Grandmother
by Mary Beth Green

Born in 1950 in St. Paul, Minnesota,
Mary Beth Green is an educator
and lives in Bozeman, Montana.

I am a genealogist, my family's historian, and among my most treasured family artifacts is a letter that came to me forty, or more, years ago, and I've read it dozens of times. The letter was written by my great-grandmother, Mary Larsen Brack. The letter is postmarked from St. Paul, Minnesota, her hometown, on November 11, 1918: Armistice Day.

She wrote the letter to her son: my grandfather, Lawrence. He was training in an Army camp in Rockford, Illinois. The letter is simple with family news, but it also contains a piece of history. My grandmother didn't know that when she posted her letter the war would end that day.

That same year, the Great Pandemic occurred: the 1918 Spanish Flu.

In the letter, my great-grandmother Mary refers to her daughter Elsie, who at the time was close to 20-years-old and was living at the family home and working. My great-grandmother writes: "Elsie has been sick lately, and we thought it was the flu, but she is feeling better now." She goes on to state that the schools in St. Paul are closed, adding, "Pa would keep the kids home anyway."

This is not a dramatic story, but it is eventful, just like the time we are living through now is eventful, different as that may be for each of us.

What I take from my great-grandmother's 1918 letter, after knowing the life span and history of each member of that family now, over 100 years later, is that they all lived through the pandemic of that time. They took care of themselves and each other as best they could and never looked back.

Grandpa Lawrence and his brother Neil were both in the Army, living in barracks, in the thick of the virus. They came home unscathed, fortunate to do so. The continuity of life held fast for that family—they were some of the lucky ones.

And I am here to tell the tale.

Alone
by Sue Gust

Born in 1962 in Tampa, Florida,
Sue Gust works in Sales and Marketing
and lives in Florence, Montana.

The first problem I encountered with the COVID-19 stay-at-home orders was sleep deprivation, not totally caused by the pandemic. I was also dealing with a sick pet that required me to get up several times a night. Once awake, it was hard to not let my brain chew on what was going on. Since I have an autoimmune condition that flares when I get sleep deprived, this was a source of additional stress. I have developed some low-level anxiety about my health issues. My husband Larry is a long-haul truck driver. He is gone often for two to two and half months at a time, so I am what I call a "married single" and alone much of the time. Socially distancing, plus not knowing what to expect, was cranking up that anxiety. I was experiencing stress-induced wheezing and pressure when I breathed. My brain would immediately ask: *Is this the coronavirus disease?*

When Larry did make it home, he self-quarantined out of an abundance of caution, staying out back in the truck for two weeks. We would visit in the garage-shop for a bit several times a day, always staying six feet apart. Having him home and near to me significantly decreased my anxiety. My breathing issues cleared up and I felt great.

Quarantine had an unexpected side benefit, though. Seeing each other, but not being able to actually touch added a little spice to our reunion once quarantine was over. We may institute quarantine more often!

I've reflected several times on the many life-altering events and experiences that I've been through and witnessed from afar. They may be lesser or greater than others. Some were personal, and some were on a world scale, but they were events that made a mark on me. Besides those personal events of deaths of family and friends, marriages, births of children, the world events that come to mind are the start of the AIDS epidemic, the eruption of Mount. St. Helens, the Columbia space shuttle disaster, the assassination of John Lennon, the 1989 Loma Prieta earthquake, and 9/11.

As dramatic and traumatic as some of these were as they were happening, I lived through them. I knew one day this pandemic would be something to reflect on in the past tense. That was comforting.

My heart goes out to those who have been struggling with major hardship during this pandemic. I've heard statistics about how calls have dramatically dropped to abuse hotlines. That's a frightening thought if abuse goes up during a crisis. Some pharmacies were offering code words that could be used if someone were in danger. How effective that would be? Imagine feeling even more trapped than under normal circumstances. As to those who were working from home AND home schooling? I think we got some idea from news reporters, entertainers, celebrities and friends and coworkers who were photobombed by their children non-stop! I laugh but it had to be a new level of stress until they could figure out a new system, if they could figure out a new system.

COVID-19 has brought home the reality of "dying alone." This seems harder on those left behind and I remember that being my underlying thought when my ex (the father of my two and only children) died. We were long separated and he was living seriously down on his luck, staying at a homeless shelter for a time. He was sleeping on his brother's couch at that moment when he was rushed to the emergency room with chest pain and laboring to breathe late at night. He died alone in the ER from undiagnosed lung cancer. That was the inconsolable thought that kept repeating through my head—he was alone. It still brings me to tears even now, almost 25 years later. Perhaps it's the guilt of not being there or being able to do SOMETHING that makes the "alone" part so hard to bear. Addressing and acknowledging that guilt may be the only way to help others move through that terrible experience and loss. From the other side of the fence, I feel like we must always be alone when we die. After all, no one is going with us. I am not a card-carrying, church-going, believer per se. I believe in God, albeit, in an unorthodox way, which is to say, I don't believe he is there with each and every one of us every moment of the day, ready to help us through every trifling issue. What I do believe is we are all given power to overcome and deal with whatever comes our way—with the help of that inner power, friends, family, nature, and gratitude. I'm an optimist—there is something to learn and something to be grateful for—always!

I am so grateful that I can do without. That I know how to function without my calendar being overloaded with activities. That I can cook some things from scratch. That I know how to add and subtract without a calculator. That I know how to write a letter. That I can entertain myself without computers, game consoles, and TVs. That I understand and came from a simpler time before the internet and WIFI. That I have experienced being self-reliant and am comfortable in my own skin and being alone. We go through life thinking we need this, and we need that, to go about our lives successfully; however, this shows me how very little we truly *need*. As we go through this pandemic, not all of the skills are necessary right now but some are, and I'm glad I have them.

My advice to future generations would be to learn some of these skills. Don't take how life is, at any given point, for granted. Be proactive about experiencing different things and thinking about what you can learn from them. Whether you ever need those experiences and skills, you may find something you appreciate and enjoy and be a better person for them.

Grief and Gratitude in the Time of a Pandemic
by Jane Jelinski

Born in 1942 in Minocqua, Wisconsin, Jane Jelinski
is a retired Commissioner from Gallatin County
and lives in Bozeman, Montana.

When the pandemic hit, this old grandma was in a near-panic because my grandchildren, Maya and Sam, were in Costa Rica with their father. They needed to get back in the U.S. before travel was suspended, and then they had to travel through Seattle, the Coronavirus Disease hotspot.

At the same time, my son Adam and his Portland-based family had Alaska Airline tickets to fly to visit me in Bozeman for their Spring Break visit on March 20th. Adam's partner Tiffany said, "I'm anxious to visit your parents, but I don't want to kill them." They canceled their reservations.

Governor Bullock declared a State of Emergency on March 12, issued a Social Distancing Advisory on March 16, then issued a travel advisory on March 19.

To prepare, my husband Jack and I high-tailed it to our local Country Bookshelf to stock up on books. At Costco, we bought what we hoped was a two-week supply of groceries. We were ready for the Stay-at-Home Directive that closed all non-essential services statewide. What a nice surprise it was to learn that Montana considers liquor stores an essential service. Now we were really ready.

Here we are, still at home more than a month later, reflecting on what I am learning through this experience. There have been some pleasant surprises. This is a good time in my life to experience this pandemic, in spite of the fact that if I do contract the COVID-19 virus it will probably be fatal because I'm 78 years old. Aside from that little piece of reality, I am overwhelmed with gratitude that Jack and I are retired and don't have to go to work, that we are healthy, that we live in a comfortable house that is paid for, and that we have food and health insurance and the basic necessities. Soon Montana's erratic April weather will settle down so we can plant our garden, which will provide a pleasurable diversion from the sense of being confined. We are so very privileged. Every day journalists report the horror this pandemic is for people who live paycheck to paycheck, the thousands of workers who have lost their jobs and who have no health insurance. We watch news footage: patients crowding hospitals and bodies being stacked into semi-trailer trucks waiting to be claimed or buried in mass graves. The suffering and death is on an unprecedented global scale, and no one anywhere is immune. There is nothing I can write that is sufficient to express the magnitude of the tragedy of this pandemic.

I am so moved to discover that this practice of social distancing has ironically and unexpectedly resulted in more connection with friends and family. My siblings in Wisconsin and I have stayed connected by email about once a week for years. Now we email each other every couple of days. Jack's siblings who live in Alaska, Florida, Massachusetts, and Wisconsin, who phoned infrequently, have all phoned and enjoyed long talks since the pandemic began. Our community is in constant communication, reaching out on the neighborhood list serve with information, and generous offers of help. My daughter Kristina who lives here in Bozeman, contacts us every day to be sure we are okay.

I am also struck by another consequence of this disaster: My children, who are mature adults and have hectic lives, are enjoying being at home with their children, homeschooling, and recreating together. Working at home, not being able to travel to meetings, while challenging, has opened the opportunity for more quality time with their children.

Maybe when this pandemic is a thing of the past, employers will back off the current frenetic pace and will remake a work environment that better balances work with time for family, rest, and recreation.

My gratitude is overshadowed daily with waves of grieving, and deep sadness. My son Adam, after a long year of struggle, has been able to right his life, maintain a stable relationship with his partner, and is an enthusiastic homeschooler to his ten-year-old daughter. However, he now works in a busy Safeway store in Portland. This is precarious work, involving contact with people all day long. I am relieved to know that they have protocols in place to protect their employees with sanitation, face masks, and protective clothing, but it is still a lot of exposure, and it worries me.

My other great concern is for my 18-year-old granddaughter Maya and her classmates. This is the absolute worst time in their lives to experience this pandemic. They are going to graduate from high school next month. This significant milestone will not be celebrated with the Pomp and Circumstance of a formal ceremony attended by family or friends, but in quarantine at home with family. This generation's future is so vague and uncertain, they are being robbed of the excitement of looking forward to college, living in a dormitory, creating bonds with new friends that might last their entire lives as adults. Maya has been accepted by every college where she applied, and has been offered some scholarships. But she cannot make a choice and a commitment to any school until there is some assurance they will be open for classes by fall. Her entire generation faces the same uncertainty.

Beyond this terribly flawed transition from high school to adulthood, there is no question that when this pandemic is behind us, the recent booming economy which has just crashed, will most likely plunge into an economic depression for a long time with few job opportunities and many challenges. Rather than rushing into adulthood, to embrace their future with open arms, welcoming independence and opportunity, these young people face a deep, dark chasm of uncertainty. Will their chosen college open in the fall? Will there be deep budget cuts at the university that will limit their academic choices? When they do, at last, get access to higher education, what opportunities will they have for employment? Our society will be fundamentally altered; there will be scarcity, there will be ongoing health challenges the global health system does not yet know how to solve.

As Jack and I take our daily walk, past the closed stores, Bozeman is a ghost town. There are virtually no other people in our commercial center that was bustling with people and events just a month ago. If we do encounter anyone, they wear masks on their faces like we do. It feels dystopian, other worldly. It is too quiet, colorless. We acknowledge our privileged status and we treasure every day knowing the future will not be the same. I am awash with gratitude for what I have and with grief for what is lost. And I am full of hope that my granddaughter's generation will forgive us, and that they will acquire the expertise to repair our economy, the wisdom to heal our political divisions, and the will to develop a health care system that finally benefits us all.

Fragments Found in a Fallowed Field
by Joy LaClaire

Born in 1951 in Annapolis, Maryland,
Joy LaClaire is a Music Producer and gives interviews
for KGVM, Bozeman Community Radio,
and lives in Bozeman, Montana.

"Take a rest; a field that has rested gives a beautiful crop."
—Ovid

Nine Haikus on This First of June (2020)

The predator drones
Have flown home, circle above
Minneapolis.

White man/White House: hides.
"American carnage"* rides
Banal, evil tides.

Watch currents, not tides.
Streams within oceans, flowing
One direction, surge.

Trifectas converge.
Sea level rises, virus
Spreads unseen, now this.

White supremacists
Insist "peace without justice."
The rest cry, "Resist!"

Locked-down since March, march.
Defy curfews, pandemics,
Together at last.

Too much is too much.
The end of "May" becomes MUST
Change now, wait no more.

Straw breaks camel's back.
Long, hot summer begins. Fires
Ignite shorter nights.

First of June, streets strewn
With burnt out shops and cop cars.
Revolution Now!

EINE KLEINE RNA

It's just a little RNA,
All un-contained,
Now run-away,
Willy-nilly holding sway
From poor house
To white house,
From your house
To my house.

Such a clever little RNA,
Not alive,
Thus so hard to kill,
Sneakily spreading
Sans symptoms
For weeks
Or months
Or years,
All around the world,
From there
An now,
To here.

Just a little RNA,
Silently riding
While hiding
Host to host,
Immune to magic
And boast.

Just a little RNA,
Unconcerned by
The Big Guy's
"bluster & blunder,"
The rest of us
Left to wonder

How we failed the test
To be able to test,

Not to mention
All the rest.

In Spain they are bleaching the beaches.
But now, they've apologized.
In the midst of the bird-breeding season,
How could they not have realized?

The children let loose in Madrid and Cadiz, on
Skate boards and bikes they careen.
Grown-ups huff and puff to keep up
With as much chance as Winter
Slowing down Spring.

The president suggests
We might self-disinfect,
It seems a good notion to him.
Then he retreats
To his tweets and retweets,
As his second term prospects grow grim.

First he said, "it's a hoax,"
Then amid all his boasts,
He claims sarcasm,
"You can't take a joke?"

It gets harder to laugh
After each foolish gaff,
Or maybe t'is meant to provoke.

While we wait
For the miracle
Of April.

IN THIS COUNTRY

In this country,
We learn geography
By invading foreign lands.

In this country,
We learn calculus
From daily exponential growth of
Death counts on graphs.

In this country,
You can fool
Some of the people
All of the time.

In this country,
When money talks,
It doesn't walk.
It flies faster than
The speed of sound
On private jets,
Socially distances
On yachts.

In this country,
"United States"
Has come to mean
Every state stands alone,
Competing with the others
To survive.

In this country,
The Commander in Chief's
Gut trumps science,
The evidence,
Common sense.

In this country,
The Buck never stops
At his desk,
No matter how reckless
He gets.

In this country,
We get the news
On late-night comedy shows.
But who's laughing now?

In this country,
It's hard to separate
News that's fake
From true.

In this country,
What can one do?

Social Distancing Was Always My Style
by Terry Lankutis

*Standing at the doors to St. Anne's Church
in Vilnius, Lithuania.*

Born in 1956, Terry Lankutis
is retired and currently manages the
family ranch in rural Montana.

Social distancing has always been a normal part of my very comfortable rural lifestyle.

In April of 2019, the day before my 63rd birthday, I was informed I had won a two thousand dollar travel voucher from a Senior Center raffle ticket. Best birthday present ever! I am full blood Lithuanian and have always thought about going to Lithuania. This winning was the motivation I needed to pursue that notion of visiting the "old country."

After diligent research, I decided to book my travel in March of 2020. My niece lives in Israel so why not add that in and visit her? A friend of mine has always wanted to visit France, so why not? She was excited to come along so the month long trip was settled. Spend a few days in France, head to Lithuania, explore and meet "new" cousins, then head off to Israel. Exciting times for a once in a lifetime trip to create many memories.

As plans began to materialize, and events of the world unfolded, I began to be grateful for the times in my past that I have had to rely on inner strength to remain positive in body, mind and spirit. I have an uncanny ability to put mind over matter and this helps keep dis-ease at bay. I found myself repeating a mantra a yoga instructors taught: "There is no place in my body for dis-ease to hide."

The first world event to challenge this ability of mine came in December 2019 when Paris had the longest transportation strike in three decades. We began to wonder if we were going to be able to get to Paris and if so, what would it be like when we got there? Would we be able to get out? Then the COVID-19 virus began to surface in China and was slowly moving to other parts of the world. Should we risk travel? After consulting with travel agents, doctors, and deep within ourselves, we were going ahead with the trip.

Plans made, all apartments booked, several day tours on our list and bags packed, our excitement level was at a very high peak, but in the back of our minds was a black cloud in the form of anxiety, uncertainty, and fear surrounding the news of a very contagious, deadly virus. I've always been one who is aware of the value of frequent handwashing, which became a habit during my days of playing in the dirt on the ranch as a child, and in my adult life during my 20 years of teaching. It's just a good thing to do. I am aware of safe ways to cough, sneeze, and distance myself so I felt I was well equipped to take on this trip during this time of crisis. I have traveled a great deal in my life. I was honest with myself about the risk I was taking, but I refused to buy into the fear mongering I felt was prevalent. Frequent deep breathing accompanied by restorative yoga and affirmations of gratitude became my constant companions.

The week we were due to leave, my travel companion made the decision not to go. Not because of the COVID-19, but due to a different health issue. Therefore, I would be taking my first international trip solo. Another opportunity for fear to rear its ugly head. I felt like I had those creatures that you see depicted on a person's shoulders, good on one side, bad on the other. I was constantly trying to push that bad one off and just pay attention to the good one. Until after the trip was over, I hadn't realized the amount of energy it took to keep looking on "the bright side of life" as Monty Python would say.

I made the decision to forgo time in France, and go directly to Lithuania and spend more time there then on to Israel. The time in Lithuania was amazing. To stand on the ground of my ancestors was emotional.

This certainly helped distract me from the looming pandemic and as I began to hear stories of how the people in the USA were beginning to panic and hoard, I was so grateful to be in a country that seemed to be taking it all in stride. I didn't wish to speculate as to why the reactions in the two countries were so different, but instead, made the choice to be grateful that I was in the country I was during the onset of this event.

I wrote a daily e-journal and took hundreds of photos. My days were overflowing with new experiences of Lithuanian culture that filled my soul. I was more content than I have been in years, possibly ever. Certainly the daily choices I was making to go out and enjoy what the country had to offer were helping me live in gratitude, rather than fear or panic.

My niece in Jerusalem and I were in constant contact regarding the idea of traveling to Israel. Travel restrictions were surfacing and flights were starting to be canceled. Living in the moment became something that was the only way to survive the unpredictability. It seemed planning ahead was becoming obsolete as the restrictions were changing on a daily, sometimes hourly, basis. I received a cancellation notice from the photographer I was to spend an afternoon with in Tel Aviv, which became the sign to forgo the trip to Israel.

If there was a turning point in the trip, this was probably it. I believe that in every moment of our lives we make choices. This was one of those moments. My niece and I chose to believe we are postponing my trip, not canceling it. Yes, I was disappointed and sad, but it was a choice as to how I would let those emotions manifest.

The most striking irony of this whole adventure was to be in Lithuania, a country which has historically experienced so much persecution, first from Stalin, then from Hitler. If my ancestors could survive being in concentration camps, being forced to survive in train cars to Siberia, then I was certainly capable of dealing with this knowing that their deep understanding of what it really takes to survive is well within my grasp. I only needed to understand that I have the ability to make choices as to my thoughts and those thoughts are directly related to my feelings and my overall health and well being.

I cut the trip short by one week. By March 15 it became obvious that if I didn't leave Lithuania by the 16th, I wouldn't know when I would be able to leave. The uncertainty took its toll on my enthusiasm and energy, so I booked flights back to the USA with underlying gratitude for the last 13 days and fierce hope that I will return one day.

My trip back was positive, though exhausting. Reflecting back, I asked myself did I make it so by focusing only on those people who were willing to help? Was it the deep breathing and the willingness to be grateful which allowed me to have the experience of a lifetime? Did I create a valuable filter, which allowed me to sift through all the information coming my way, and internalize only what was necessary to make informed decisions? The answers to these questions are all a resounding yes. The phrase "the power of positive thinking" might seem like an old cliche, but oftentimes I find deep wisdom in what we consider "old."

It is common practice for me to ask myself what can I, or have I, learned from a particular event. The unique experience with this for me has been the element of unpredictability. For the most part, I can make plans, and even though, as in this case, the trip was very different than originally planned, I was able to know that I could plan to leave on a certain day, get to my destination, and take part in activities each day. But once everything became so unpredictable, not knowing what the next hour or day would bring, was a new feeling for me.

Thus, once again, I was led to gratefulness. I have never felt that I take my lifestyle for granted. I know how lucky I am to have a roof over my head, meals on my table, and even toilet paper in my closet each day. There are so many people in this world who live each and every day with this feeling of unpredictability. That is their normal. My hope for them is that as a result of these world events, there is new realization that some might NOT want to return to their normal. That new awareness causes us all to take a hard look at our lives and see what effect our daily choices have on our lives and on those around us.

The Plague Diaries
by Kimberlee Lawrence

Born in 1950 in Montana, Kimberlee Lawrence
is a writer, a former librarian, preschool teacher,
and lives in Stevensville, Montana.

I was five years old when I first heard the word quarantine. I demanded to know what it meant. It sounded magical.

My mother gave a clear definition, but I was a detail girl who wanted more details. *Why would people be separated just because they were sick? How sick do you have to be? Can it ever happen to us?*

That's not magical! The notion of quarantine offended me.

Before MMR (Measles, Mumps, and Rubella) vaccinations, before Drs. Sabin and Salk saved my generation, I visualized familiar diseases—colds, stomach flu. My mom showed me her small pox vaccination and pointed out mine. She told me that terrible diseases used to kill people. Before the shot which keeps us safe, small pox caused quarantines. This probably was when she first told me about the Spanish Flu pandemic.

My house in Stevensville, Montana was the last on our street and was adjacent to the cemetery. The cemetery was my park—the nearest place with deciduous trees, the only decent ones to lean against to read, the only place to pile up leaves for jumping and burrowing. A cemetery can also be a source of companionship for the preferentially solitary. Mine was a boy neighborhood. When the boys were boring, I read tombstones.

In one section I discovered clusters of people—children, parents, dead within days of each other. I knew why from the dates.

Many children's graves were marked by simple marble tablets, some with a statue of a lamb reclining on top. The white marble sparkled in the sun, but rusty patches of lichens streaked across inscriptions, discolored the lambs. No one visited these graves on Memorial Day. No one polished the stones or left flowers. So I did.

Mom was home because Dad's law office was closed for Friday court sessions. I invited her for a walk. We picked sprigs of lilacs from bushes surrounding our house and I took her to visit my friends. We passed rotted-off wooden grave markers leaning against the fence that bordered the ranch lane. We slipped through trailing strands of the weeping willow. I gathered the shriveled lilac blooms of Memorial Day and exchanged them for fresh. It was then I noticed my mother crying quietly over the lambs. "So many," she whispered. "So young. Some just babies."

We read inscriptions to each other, sharing heartbreak expressed in stone. We left the lambs, scouting deeper into the section to find similar graves—young adults, grandparents, surnames scattered among other surnames, dead on similar dates. No time for family plots. Stevensville's losses were too high for that.

Random death became my theme for life. The 1950s parental polio panic led first to pink sugar cubes, then to shots for immunity. There were the Bitterroot Valley's annual "tick shot" clinics, like those for polio, held in the high school gyms. These staved off Rocky Mountain spotted fever, another potential death threat deeply ingrained in local culture. Spotted fever had managed to nearly kill my mother's mom and my father's dad. Considerable disease and death tales were dredged deep into my childhood lore.

Hanging out in cemeteries led to a college term paper on the Black Death. Later came a short story about lamb tombstones and the children who lay beneath them. It's probably the reason I've spent twenty years writing about war. Mom's taste for the macabre, plus all this background in disease and death has resulted, to my extreme amazement, in my living through a time of contagion under quarantine.

Behold, I possess the perfect background and temperament for it!

At five, I thought it unspeakable to be shut away in our little house, all of us locked in together, no escaping outside to play. Far too much togetherness with my contentious family. Unthinkable!

That was then. This is now.

I live the same life I lived before lock down, quietly isolated with TV and computer. All that changed is I go to church by video and in my pajamas. I spend many days in pajamas because my food obsessed husband is overfeeding us. My jeans fit, but tightly. Pajamas are more comfy for quarantines.

My house is a bit more spacious than that one long ago. Instead of five of us packed together in the quarantine I imagined in that tiny house with one bathroom, my husband and I enjoy elbow room a mile away. There are TV's in this world. At five years old in 1954, I was blissfully ignorant of television. We boast two bathrooms, too—even if there's just enough toilet paper for one.

As a 70-year-old, I notice NBC's lovely Kate Snow grow more haggard as days pass. Her husband has a mild case of the virus, self-isolating in the guest bedroom and bath. She works from home, cares for his needs, cleans obsessively, and homeschools. In a group interview of other mothers, she admits to being too sharp with her kids and beginning to drink too much. I don't blame her. When I consider myself in the shoes of those women, I know I'd be a raving lunatic.

I'm fortunate. Those New York City mothers suspect viruses swirl around every concrete corner. I sit holed up in my office with a view of my mountains, walled off as if my life were like theirs—but in Montana's relative safety. I'm a vicarious participant in their pandemic. They are justly afraid. I am not. They suffer to keep the virus at bay, to flatten the curve, to prevent further spread. I'm mostly catching up on the backlog in my DVR.

I have another advantage—being older. Motherhood's accountabilities lessen with age. I text my children, urge them to stay indoors, avoid friends. I remind them to check their temperatures. I don't worry that they probably ignore me. They are adults, likely better at this all this than I. They can handle it on their own, as was my plan. I raised them with the realities that death lurks behind every bush. I know they are more prepared for life than are their friends raised to adulthood with gentler family stories.

My husband of 49 years is resigned to the fact that I'm essentially a hermit. I've made him into one. For entertainment he forages for food and toilet paper. Surprisingly, he's learned to interpret Scottish brogue laced with Gaelic after bingeing three seasons of "Outlander" with me—an intellectual curiosity for which I never would have credited him in the past.

Together we ponder our situation. We agree—and we rarely hold the same point of view on *anything*—that those who demand swift opening of the country aren't facing reality. Currently in New York, one person dies of COVID every two minutes. COVID-19's westward trek has hardly begun. Fewer than 300 tests have been conducted in our entire state. The time to turn people loose on the streets is still months in the future.

The effort Americans made to isolate should count for more than a postponement of spread. Economic impact is less painful for seniors than for younger families, but to keep all families healthy, leaders must face sober facts. We may well endure another historic element from our past—a reprise of the Great Depression. But more of us will live. Life, not money, should be the highest priority.

We burrow together, my husband and I, both immune-compromised. He searches Fox for enlightenment and I, watch MSNBC and—more death—my true crime channels. We continue to overlook each other's quirks with the same patient irritation that has kept us from strangling each other for all these years.

We regard each other with kind eyes and totally agree.

We live in interesting times.

A Bow and an Outbreath
by D Jan Matney

Born in 1948 in Hamlin, Texas, D Jan Matney
is the Director of The Center Counseling and Neurofeedback
and lives in Bozeman, Montana.

My husband and I moved to Bozeman in 1974 and over the next ten years we had three children. I consider us all, our children and grandchildren, Montanans.

I came here, dreams in tow, before this was the next Aspen or Jackson Hole and before everyone knew the name 'Bozeman'. Back then, friends and acquaintances outside our state asked me how I liked living in Wyoming. Montana and Wyoming were the same. I followed a dream of living in the Rocky Mountains, and in return, I found beauty and good friends. My husband and I birthed babies at home, and later took them to church, and when they were old enough, we put them in inner tubes to float the Madison River. I lived in this small town, until finally, immersed in our culture, I, too, began grasping and reaching for more, more travel and restaurants, more self-help books and workshops, often left unread. The high-rise buildings going up, too numerous to count, did not bother me. There was no Bozeman to save because I was part of the 'push' endemic to our culture. Life was full and rich in many ways, but without the time to contemplate what I was doing and why.

They say time is not linear, and I do remember when time stretched out differently. Then, there was young motherhood, sitting on the front steps of our house, watching the evening close, chatting with neighbors, laughing. But after some deliberation, I took a detour, and I mark it happening when we moved, three small children and my husband and I, into a house with three floors. They say children can't navigate large houses; they become untethered. That's one thing, the house, but I married that same large house with a mission: graduate school, trainings, long nights. Despite my best intentions, I felt absorbed by the house and the mission, which seemed to have a life of their own.

When Montana's Governor Steve Bullock said "stop," stay at home, quarantine, I did. I was fearful, but I couldn't deny the huge outbreath I was required to make with this change. We were all required. For the first time in years, I cooked, ate well at our kitchen table, and listened to my husband (not always my forte). I slowed. Marie Kondo became my personal favorite advisor. I found what mattered most to me now was the same as when I lived in our small house: a quieter, kinder self who had time. I started reading again and watching TV and going for bike rides and walks—organizing my internal and external worlds as though they mattered—as though I mattered.

These past two months, I've had time to question and to consider my dreams (the ones at night), and beyond that, consider that I could be receiving messages not only from my unconscious, but from spirits. I can only hope. I've read and reread an explanation of the double slit experiment until I could hold a thought about quantum mechanics and then hold some more thoughts about what quantum mechanics implies. I've raked my yard, planted flowers, played peek-a-boo with my granddaughter, asked our daughter to go on a walk, then leisurely waited for her to do mom stuff at her house. I'm considering making chicken enchiladas either tonight or tomorrow with no concern about what such an investment of my time could mean. Good Mexican food is a gift.

It's amazing how something so tiny and invisible—a bit of genetic material not technically alive—can change so much for everyone. We are talking science fiction that the whole world could shut down because of this inert, smaller than small thing, complete with a halo surrounding it—hence the coronavirus disease. People have died from it, and we all remain at risk. I imagine this viral insult will have a resurgence of its power in time. I doubt it's over. So how should we navigate such an unwanted connection? For me, I would wish to hold to a modicum of outbreath, to a recognition of viral power, and a bow to the "awe-fulness" of life.

Staying Home in "The Last Best Place"
by Jackie Montgomery

Born in 1937 in Britton, South Dakota,
Jackie Montgomery is a retired teacher and church secretary
and lives in Bozeman, Montana.

Most stressful about staying in place for me is missing in-person interaction with longtime friends! Modern technology helps us communicate, but as a people person, I miss hugs, laughter, and facial expressions. My husband, R.G., and I, celebrating our 60th anniversary, have always been best friends, as well as spouses, so we share feelings freely. Physically, we can go out in public while practicing safe precautions, but limit that to only necessary tasks. I, particularly, having grown up on a farm on the Dakota Prairie in the 40s and 50s, am experienced at staying home, being prepared, and finding activities for days on end. With our three young families living far away we are accustomed to joining them only annually.

R.G. and I read many books about history. Lately, I've compared our worries with conditions during the Revolutionary War, when people were divided in loyalty between our fledgling country and England, fighting over federal or state rights, waging a war, experiencing poverty, and experiencing the arrival of a smallpox epidemic when immunization was still scary and experimental. My early days were imprinted with effects of the Great Depression, World War II, and fear of polio. Similarities with today? Yes! I cling to a mantra, "This, too, shall pass!"

Our current dilemma involves a midway halt for us to move from Bozeman to Wisconsin where our daughter lives. We have a senior-friendly apartment rented there and, with family, had a plan to move this summer. As do-it-yourself folks, we planned to rent a large U-Haul truck and our sons lovingly offered to help pack, drive, and unpack. However, they would need to fly from California and Texas in danger of contracting COVID-19 and inadvertently spreading it to their families. This concerns us all, especially our daughter, an epidemiologist. We've abandoned that plan for the time being and are in an extended, wait-and-see period, especially with daily projections of increase in spread of the disease, no vaccine yet, and rightfully-so, restrictions on travel between states.

As R.G. and I have gotten older, our decision to move nearer family rose from wishing to give up home maintenance and realizing possible need of assistance due to health limitations in the future. For months we worked through the "grieving leaving Bozeman" which evolved into excitement about beginning a new life chapter. Then the COVID-19 pandemic arrived mid-March! We are experiencing an emotional roller-coaster while packing boxes, readying the house for sale, and donating, selling, recycling and discarding stuff accumulated over a half-century. I am keeping a progress record in Margareta Magnusson's book *The Gentle Art of Swedish Death Cleaning*; it's a primer for streamlining life while counting joys through memories embedded in things.

Although it is disconcerting to feel psychologically in two places simultaneously, we are healthy, enjoy many hobbies, and have a comfortable home and plenty to eat. As a planner with limited patience, I get frustrated being unable to calendar our future, but then, I think of people who are suffering in so many ways and am reminded of my blessings. Trained as an elementary education teacher, I sympathize greatly with teachers and parents struggling to help children learn while sheltering in place, working from home, or working out of the home as an essential worker. As a retired full-time church secretary, I'm aware of the deep spiritual needs of many, while I work to maintain my own faith when separated from our beloved congregation.

Additional uneasiness comes from a desire to volunteer to help in some way, but limited as one in the "vulnerable" age group. Fortunately, I found enough fabric and thread from packed boxes to make two dozen face masks for our extended family. For me that was a different way to spend Holy Week. I am learning to be more gracious about kindnesses as receivers, rather than thanks as givers. How odd to have so much time, often desired, and then not being able to settle into an activity. I find myself moving saved furniture and decor from one place to another to fill empty wall spaces which bother me.

I hope we all, especially young people, realize our blessings, cherish relationships, find ways to help others, and appreciate lessons enabling us to be compassionate leaders in the post-pandemic world.

Each year I write a genealogy chapter for our extended family based on old letters, research, scrapbooks, and photo albums. At the end of last year, I chose the current title "What If" to describe choices, good luck, and wonderful people in our life journey. I compare that story with what might have happened through other possibilities. Little did I expect to conclude with this "What If" facing us in 2020!

Resilience for a Dark Age
by Susan Morgan

Born in 1937 in New London, Connecticut,
Susan Morgan is a retired Clinical Social Worker
and Diplomate Jungian Psychoanalyst
and lives in Bozeman, Montana.

During this challenging time of COVID-19 and the suffering of so many, my life has not changed outwardly that much. I spent the winter in solo meditation retreat at my house and am an introvert by nature so that for the first time in my life, the world is doing what I love to do and I am in the majority. My family is very supportive and gets my groceries for me. I haven't been anywhere for a month except to walk the dogs and get the mail. I meditate, write, play a lot of solitaire and watch Netflix. The house is warm, the wood stove crackles away, and carrot soup simmers on the stove. There is a stunning disconnect between my daily life and the disruption, pain, and uncertainty in the world. Underneath my comfortable daily life, the stress, suffering, and anxiety of our time breaks my heart open. At times, the anxiety churns in my body for myself, my loved ones, and all the suffering world.

Buddha said, "There is suffering. Why would I think suffering is an aberration? Old age, sickness, and death is our lot. Ancient and immutable laws." Maybe we are stricken because we think it can't happen here. Not to us. Not in America. We think we can overcome adversity if we work hard enough, if we do it "right," if we figure it out, if we are good, creative. I think like this, still, to a degree, but I was born in 1937. Hitler was coming to power. World War II disrupted my young life, laying a traumatic foundation for me. I studied history, read the Bible, the story of wars, conflict, and every form of strife, plagues. These are human conditions, along with the joys and happinesses. Ten thousand joys. Ten thousand sorrows. I cry for us all and our beloved country and sense the fragility and precariousness of our lives. The coronavirus disease shows that life rests on a single breath.

The Buddha says that there is an end to suffering. He taught remedies that we can rely on, such as seeking understanding instead of judging, setting noble goals, speaking and acting with care, be mindful and calm the mind.

The uncertainty of these times opens up the possibility for a creative response to the great challenges we face: endemic poverty, decline of American democracy, and global climate change. This can be a time of deep introspection into the shadow of our culture and ourselves and we can turn from the false god of materialism. The virus has demonstrated that we are all connected, connected by the invisible dots of virus and by the necessity of working together in our shared common humanity. In the horror of the moment, there is outpouring support for the front-line workers: nurses, doctors, grocery clerks, delivery people, the essential ones. We can show support and compassion for them; compassion arising for those suffering with the virus, the dying, the families of the suffering and dead, those stuck at home with small children, in abusive relationships, losing jobs, going stir crazy with the isolation and fear.

What can I do? As I age, I'm not as active in the community as I used to be. I can send small amounts of money to food banks and support progressive politicians, feed the birds, call my friends. What I find most helpful are two practices that ground me and help me open my heart. It doesn't do any good to be stuck in the morass. First. Pause. Breathe. Pausing and breathing.

These two simple immediate things have gotten me through many a tough spot. Stop. Breathe into the gut, the lungs, feel the breath in the body. Take one second. Notice the pulsing, churning sensations or whatever you are feeling, and without thinking, watch it, watch it do its thing, dissipate, dissolve. Then there is a practice I do for myself, others and the world: Tonglen. It also involves breathing. I see myself, loved ones, the suffering ones, the world sorrow before me.

Experience the distress, breathe it in as smoke. Let the heart open and breath out love, compassion, healing. Light. Bring light into the world in the perfect moment between hope and despair. Clear light.

Ultimately, it's experience things just as they are. I am an old privileged white woman. I haven't had to close my restaurant business like my nephew, I am not a hospital nurse like my friend, Mary, and I haven't been deathly sick with the virus like my friend Sue. But I will say for myself and the younger generations and all the children of this dark time, we are larger than the fear of our reptilian brains. Have confidence. We can be held by our larger selves in love and compassion. Life is larger than we often know. We are larger. This year of COVID-19 will pass. It may be a dress rehearsal for the difficult future we likely face with climate change. We have amazing resources within us. We have an infinite source of love, compassion, courage, and wisdom. May we use these qualities in ourselves and in each other—our boundless, spacious, open-hearted being—for the benefit of all beings.

My Response to the Pandemic
by Mary R. Nelson

Born in 1939 in Butte, Montana,
Mary R. Nelson is a retired librarian
and lives in Florence, Montana.

Elder: A person of advanced age, ancient, geriatric, old-timer, senior citizen. I don't think about these designations too much, until I look in a mirror. What a shock! I wonder if anyone will be interested or pay any attention to "my wisdom."

I am 81 years old. I grew up on a ranch near Wisdom, Montana in the Big Hole Basin and attended a one-room school where I was the only one in my grade. When I was 11, we moved to Anaconda and my class size was 30. I met my husband while a student at the University. Don worked for the Forest Service and we moved eight times during his career. While we traversed the country, I earned three degrees: a B.A. in History, a B.A. in Education, and a Masters in Library and Information Science. I particularly enjoyed working in the Agency for International Development Library while in the DC area. We both retired in 1996 and live in the Bitterroot Valley.

I find myself sequestered in a beautiful place, we have a wonderful view of the mountains and a creek bubbling back of our house. Actually what more could I ask for?

In early March, the Pandemic didn't seem too relevant to me; China was a long way from Montana. It didn't occur to me to wonder how the Coronavirus disease would affect me, so I was surprised when my daughter, a doctor, called and said we shouldn't go to Spokane on March 12 to see our grandson perform with his College Collegiate Chorale.

As the news came from TV, newspapers, internet; local, state, and national, I felt a certain amount of disbelief, life as I would never have imagined; very unreal as things were coming to an abrupt stop. These great unknowns. How long will this go on? What can I do? Where can I go? Our lives are very different now. Previously unknown concepts are now a new norm: safe distancing, face masks. Schools, stores, restaurants, businesses, fitness centers, hair and nail salons all closed. Stay at home, WASH your hands, sanitize!

Now as the reality has sunk in, my next emotion is one of compassion, for all those really suffering from loss of jobs and all that entails, for the homeless and for those who are ill, and the loss of life.

People's lives are being turned upside down. Closures of churches, schools, sporting events, entertainment venues, no travel, no graduations, nor visiting our friends and neighbors. This has become the new norm! Students being out of school and studying at home doesn't work for all of them because the great economic divide doesn't provide computers, tablets, or other electronic items to all families. I hate to think how COVID will affect education at all levels.

There is another piece of this whole terrible time that causes me much anguish. That is the political scene; it is very unsettling to have a President who is completely clueless; he makes terrible and stupid remarks. And he has no empathy! To me that is one of the most important characteristics for people in leadership roles (and actually for all humans).

Physically: I'm dealing with a "new" health problem. I have talked to my doctor on the phone, but getting a blood test at the hospital sounds scary. I'm a little paranoid about being out and about.

Psychologically: Not so good. We have things going on in our life that is causing lots of stress and angst.

Emotionally: We worry about our daughter, the doctor; I just heard yesterday she has been exposed!

Our son in Texas owns a durable medical supply business. He provides oxygen, walkers, wheel chairs, etc. His store is open and he is around lots of people. He also had to cut staff and suffers loss of income.

Spiritually: We are fine. We have a great pastor and we can watch Sunday services on YouTube. We also have our Bible Study on Zoom.

Two days later: It's sunny and what a difference that makes. I'm thinking how lucky I am. I live in a beautiful place, in my dream house with a spectacular view. The birds are chirping in the trees. Our granddaughter is coming to hang out and study. She is a bright star in our lives.

There are other joys. Our forsythia bushes are blooming in all their yellow glory. My African violets are blooming again. We have been calling friends and relatives far and wide (just received a long email from our friends in England), catching up is great. It was fun to have a Zoom Book Club to discuss, visit, and see each other.

In a way, I am enjoying not being so busy. I can do things I enjoy: long leisurely breakfasts, drinking coffee, reading the paper, doing jig saw puzzles, and reading my stack of books. I can catch up with projects, such as repotting my African violets and planting a garden.

The negatives include: not eating out, cooking in more, not being able to see grandchildren's graduations, Julie not coming to vacuum, not having my hair, toes, and nails lovingly restored by my beautiful beautician! But I am sending checks for every time we miss, and canceled sports. I'm a sports nut and if there is no football in the fall I'll be very sad.

What does the future hold? I keep hearing about a new normal. It's too early to even guess, but I'm hoping very, very much that Joe Biden becomes the President and that Steve Bullock is elected to the U.S. Senate. They aren't miracle workers, but I feel they have compassionate hearts and souls and care about all people.

Advice to future generations: be compassionate, have empathy, think of and support others, advocate and work for climate change, public land protection, human rights, immigrant and undocumented workers, and gun control. Also, support political leaders who work for the best of our country.

In short, think of others and DO GOOD. Try to be positive, enjoy the beauty of our world. Keep learning, remember the past, take the best and make the future better. BE HAPPY!

Cowgirl Up
by Pamela Niemi

Born in 1955 in Denver, Colorado,
Pamela Niemi is a critical care nurse
and lives in Las Vegas, Nevada.

I have felt the most stress psychologically. Being a nurse, I am working in an environment where we have patients with the virus and patients under suspicion for the virus. Therefore, I mentally treat every patient like they could potentially be positive for it. Meaning, I am wearing a mask, gloves, and goggles for every patient, every day, for 12 hours, only taking the garb off for lunch. It wears on my mind . . . with every patient. I don't want to get it and I definitely don't want to bring it home to my family.

Fortunately being positioned in the postanesthesia care unit (PACU), I have only had to go into a COVID room, or visit a PUI, patient under investigation for COVID, a few times. That is full on war gear: double mask, hair cover, eye goggles, plastic gown, double gloves, and shoe covers. An hour in an outfit like that and your body temperature goes up and you feel like you are filling your shoes with sweat. And when you come out, you feel dirty, like somehow it's on you.

Physically, I feel the loss of my kickboxing gym. I have no motivation to workout at home. I feel lazy. I feel tired. This whole situation is heavy and wears me down.

Spiritually, I feel like I am growing. I feel more spiritual. I'm not exactly clear what it is that I believe, but my two close workmates are very religious and we pray together. We pray for people to recover from this and we pray for our own safety and our families. It feels good. They are clear about what they believe in; however, I'm exploring. I can tell you that I have had the privilege to be with patients when they have died and I recall feeling the moment their spirit, their essence has moved on. To where, I'm not sure, but I do believe there is more to the journey.

I have so many adventures and wonderful memories to draw from, more than I can actually recall. Trips, river and land, epic parties. Good friends, soulmates, near and far.

I think of younger, simpler times that my BFF Joni and I refer to as the "Glory Days." In the Glory Days we went traveling without much thought, we accepted drinks in a bar from a person without worry, we walked alone outside at night or traveled alone, or grocery shopped at two in the morning. These days, I would be hesitant to do these things. No actually, these are things I just would not do. But it was a much simpler time in nursing. It was just nursing, not nursing productivity. There were no Press-Ganey patient satisfaction scores to get between you and providing good care of the patient.

I think a lot will be different after this pandemic. As a society, we were already isolating in some ways from texting, instead of calling to looking at our phones in public, to watching movies at home, instead of going to the theater. With every mass shooting, I felt society retreating a little bit more. After this, people will still be afraid to interact. Will we no longer hug our friends and workmates? I am a hugger by nature and tapping elbows or toes with people feels odd and impersonal. I think we will hug less.

Will the mom-and-pop stores go the way of the dinosaur? Will we only be shopping at the big commercial stores that made it through? Will Amazon dominate making Jeff Bezos even richer? Will we order our groceries, instead of going to the store. Yes, I think some will.

I hope collectively we come together as a society with more thoughts and concerns for people less fortunate. I think the pandemic will accentuate the need for this. I feel awful thinking of people and families that are struggling to pay their rent or feed their children. The women who are trapped in abusive relationships that are now even more trapped because of this situation.

My heart breaks at the thought of the patient dying alone and their families. Unimaginable. My 92-year-old father who lives in Florida was hospitalized and placed in rehab after a fall. My sister and I are unable to go because no visitors are allowed. I have horrible thoughts of him in rehab catching the virus, dying, and ending up in a refrigerated truck . . . in a parking lot. The horrible thoughts continued where I saw myself sitting outside the make-shift morgue truck, grieving that he was in there. Grieving because he was a good, kind, decent, loving man, a great Dad, and he deserved better. All the dead deserved better. All of them.

I have felt the pain and hardship of my fellow healthcare workers around the world. I weep reading the stories, like the nurse who within the first six hours of her shift had six patients die. The story of a nurse in a COVID room dressed in full gear for 12 hours with a patient so sick, inverted, on 15 drips that you cannot leave for a moment.

These stories really affect me and even though I am not there, I feel their pain. I am not there, but I feel how tired they are. I am not there, but I know how stressed they are. I feel all these things. I am not there, yet I am. I know this because in my 43 years as a Critical Care nurse, ICU, ER, and now PACU, I have experienced similar situations, but none that compare to this. Nothing compares to this, except war. When you are born into this profession, you are different. At least I am. You are universally connected. You are one.

This pandemic is psychologically draining. I feel like some days I am tired from feeling. From feeling the global pain. It feels heavy.

I feel scared. Scared when I am assigned to a possible COVID. I don't want to get it or give it to my family and friends. I feel embarrassed and weak for feeling scared. I am stronger than this, I am braver than this. Get a grip. Cowgirl up. And I do. And I do my job because that is what I am trained to do. Born to do.

After this, I will hold my friends and family closer and care less about my possessions. I will simplify.

Essential Service
by Joni Payne

Born in 1955, Joni Payne
is a Training Manager for the US Postal Service
and lives in Las Vegas, Nevada.

I currently work as a manager of training and development for the U.S. Postal Service. I am eligible for retirement, but I've decided to work another year to finance some big-ticket items on the house.

During the COVID-19 pandemic, the Postal Service was listed as an essential service for the country. The agency decided to start a hiring blitz for temporary employees to fill the gap for an affected workforce and to accommodate an increase in online shopping because states shut down retail facilities and the malls closed. This meant that our training department would provide new employee orientation to hundreds of people in our classrooms. In addition to the social distancing and protective wear guidelines, we were nervous for our own safety and health.

When Steve Sisolak, the Governor of Nevada, declared a state of emergency on March 16, 2020, it became real, professionally and personally. In the event we were approached by law enforcement during a lockdown, all postal employees were issued letters to carry with us, identifying us as essential federal employees.

In that first ten days, I woke up screaming in the middle of the night, twice. Both times, it was a stranger trying to get into a building with intent to harm. My sleep patterns were disrupted. During these night spins, I would think about how different segments of the population would be affected by this global pandemic: the newly unemployed, the homeless, the Las Vegas Strip hotel property employees, dysfunctional families forced together by stay-at-home orders, and on and on and on.

I finally had to narrow my focus on those people that I could directly help. The first being my 83-year-old, recently widowed, father who was 500 miles away. Since I was an essential employee going to work, my retired husband and I decided that I would be the designated grocery shopper to better protect the home front. And that started the adaptive rhythm for me. I'm fortunate enough to be financially stable with an income that was not affected, and so, when I could, I could help siblings with grocery gift cards, deliver staples and foodstuffs to my father, and support my friends' online businesses.

I set up my sewing machine in my home office and created a mask-making sideline project for family and friends. And when it's safe to do so, I am going to get my first tattoo: a needle and thread, to honor the women who taught me the art of sewing.

At work I tried to set a positive tone for the training team and make sure that we had adequate protective equipment and followed the CDC and agency guidelines. New trainees that were not compliant with these guidelines were asked to leave. It's been a very stressful time with the busy training schedule, having to wear masks, and adhere to social distancing.

Even though I haven't been to church since I was 17, I credit my Mormon upbringing with its practice of self-reliance and home food and supply storage with my own practice of stocking my pantry with surplus sundry items. My hope is that people learn the important lesson of preparation, so that they don't resort to panic shopping and hoarding as part of their plan, but instead are able to adapt with less stress and spend their energy on helping others during crisis times like this.

Spring Fever Virus
by Carolyn Pinet

Born in 1943 in Milford Haven, South Wales,
United Kingdom, Carolyn Pinet is a retired
Spanish Professor and lives in Bozeman, Montana.

"Overflowing as ever, the world awaits me."
—Jorge Guillen, Cantico

They're back—
I just looked, saw a tail feather
sticking out of the nest
and thought, "There go the robins,
indefatigable, cock-eyed optimists"—
they knew that spot by the back-door was,
to put it mildly, iffy,
but here they are, another heady spring,
and drunk on their hormones—do birds
have hormones?—
undaunted by the lessons of the past,
they have built yet another nest,
the female has laid her eggs,
and they await the hatch.

What is it about the Montana spring?
Even the elders among us
feel jaunty and restless

despite dire warnings, troubled times.
Is it that we have learned nothing so
are doomed to repeat our missteps,
or is it, like the robins,
we are wildly disposed
to start over, flit about,
inhale the redolent blossoms
and to love this world?

Pandemic Journal: Birds & Revolutions Included
by Adele Pittendrigh

Born in 1946 in Charlottesville, Virginia,
Adele Pittendrigh is a retired Associate Dean
and lives in Bozeman, Montana.

May 5, 2020: I got up early this morning and met two friends to go out birding. This would be the first time I'd done anything at all with friends since March 12th when the pandemic was officially announced and we started sheltering-in-place. We headed to Three Forks, Montana, in separate cars, wore face masks when walking, and maintained social distancing.

We saw a lot of birds but the showiest were two White-faced Ibis, large shore birds with luscious opalescent green and rust bodies and a white feathered outline around red faces. They have long yellow downturned bills and red legs. These birds are muscular and strong. The ancient Egyptians associated the African Ibis with Thoth, the god of writing, magic, and wisdom. They depicted Thoth with an Ibis head and mummified millions of them. Seriously, there is research about whether all these mummified Ibis were raised on farms or were wild birds. It looks like they were more likely wild birds.

Today the *Bozeman Daily Chronicle* published an opinion piece by David Brooks about the pandemic entitled, "Reflecting on the Pain, Building a New Future." He writes, "The pandemic has been a massive humanizing force—allowing us to see each other on a level much deeper than politics—see the fragility, the fear and the courage."

Will the pandemic help bring us all together as human beings? Will we be kinder to each other? Will racism and hatred decline? Maybe a change is coming. Maybe later on we'll talk about this time as a turning point and we'll talk about the Pre- and Post- COVID-19 Eras.

May 17, 2020: This morning, I can hear from the kitchen Pine Siskins make their loud, rising *tzeee* call. At the feeder are two Pine Siskins with an American Goldfinch, and this goldfinch takes my breath away, especially in early morning light when its dazzling yellow seems to glow from within.

This pandemic has me on an emotional roller coaster: sometimes the birds make me happy, or something else gives me joy, but then horrible news will come about the pandemic.

Note to Self for the Pandemic:
Keep your balance. Take deep breaths. Notice something
    beautiful every day. Walk every day.
Do not watch TV news until further notice. Read news
    from reputable sources.
Keep track of the numbers. How many new cases?
    How many dead?

What would we do if the trustworthy press—the ones that do research, seek facts, and use reason—did not (or could not) do their job, and we were in the dark about everything? How would we make it through the pandemic if all we had to go on were confusions, lies, and chaos?

Today *The Washington Post* reports that 87,000 people dead in the US by COVID-19 virus and at least 1,458,000 cases reported in the nation.

May 18, 2020: This morning, it's lightly overcast at 6:30 a.m. A Black-Billed Magpie and a White-Crowned Sparrow are hopping around each other under the feeder eating seeds that fell on the ground. The magpie is maybe eight times bigger than the sparrow. Usually, small birds fly away when there is a magpie nearby, but this one doesn't fly when the magpie moves toward it. It's as though they are equals and maybe the sparrow feels this is his back yard, too. Or, that the magpie is the interloper. They do their very active feeding dance for a while, and then, the sparrow makes a run toward the magpie and the magpie flies off. Headline: SPARROW TROUNCES MAGPIE!

May 19, 2020: I got up at 6 a.m. and drove about five miles to go on a bird walk. The trail goes through a lovely woodland that has a pond, meets up with a river, and then circles back to the place I parked my car. Today there was no one but me on the trail.

Walking through these woods in May in the early morning is like walking inside a music box made by God and angels. A whole chorus of birds is singing and I am just now during this pandemic time learning to separate and identify individual birds by their songs. Once the weather warmed up, I walked every day and I was amazed at how well I could identify the birds by their songs alone. I thought I had really made progress on something I'd been working on for years—learning to identify birds from their songs. My friend pointed out that perhaps I hear the separate songs better because it's so quiet. Few planes are flying and there's much less traffic when everyone is sheltering in place. No wonder I can hear.

Some good news from the pandemic today from *The Washington Post* headline reads: *Global Emissions Plunged an Unprecedented 17 Percent During the Coronavirus Pandemic.* When people started staying home the amount of driving, flying, and producing stuff plummeted. There was a decline of more than 1 billion tons of carbon dioxide emissions into the atmosphere. As a result of the decline, the folks who conducted the study predict the total decline in greenhouse emissions for 2020 will be down between 4% and 7% at year's end. The news is good because we need to reduce emissions a lot this year and for the years to come if humankind is to avoid the worst effects of climate change.

Is it possible the pandemic will give us a taste for clear skies and clean air? Could we, as we start up the economy, promote clean energy and aim for a healthier atmosphere and healthier planet?

May 21, 2020: I didn't go birding today. It was cold and windy, and there's a winter storm warning for 9 p.m. tonight through noon on Friday. I went to the Garden Center to see if the Black Krim tomato plants were in yet. They weren't.

Then my husband and I decided to get some coffee and muffins in one of our favorite places to get such things. Montana is opening up after all, and it's been a long time since we stopped for coffee and a treat. We were surprised though when we saw that the young people working behind the long display case were not wearing masks. I asked, "Why don't you all wear masks?" The answer was, "Our boss doesn't think it's necessary." We took our muffins and coffee to the car. But those workers had to stay there and interact with anyone who came into the restaurant. They had no protection, not even a Plexiglass shield in front of the cash register. It looks like health precautions are taking their place in the culture wars.

Today, *The New York Times* published a useful article for people interested in regulations that protect and preserve the environment and human health, entitled "The Trump Administration is Reversing 100 Environmental Rules." The article reports that the rollbacks "repealed and replaced Obama-era emissions rules for power plants and vehicles; weakened protections for more than half the nation's wetlands; and withdrew the legal justification for restricting mercury emissions from power plants."

This article provides an easy-to-use guide to all the 100 environmental rules that are being reversed, with detailed explanations of their purpose and history. One rule trashes the Migratory Bird Treaty Act (MBTA), which was signed in 1918 to protect birds from extinction. It has been the most important regulation for protecting birds for over 100 years. The new rule is that if the killing of migratory birds is unintentional, it is not prohibited. Now if you kill birds unintentionally you will not be fined by the federal government. This is a gift to oil companies who may kill millions of birds in a big oil spill.

Ironically, during the time of this pandemic when we all want good health, the current administration is scurrying to reverse 100 environmental rules, forty-six of which are in categories that definitely affect our health: air pollution, toxic substances and safety regulations, and water pollution.

May 24, 2020: This morning when I woke up, it was rainy and cold again. I saw a red fox running across the field. It was zigzagging fast up the hill. I went to get my binoculars but it was gone by the time I got back.

In Montana our Governor, Steve Bullock, directed Montanans to stay home early enough to prevent the disease from spreading widely. We were allowed to travel for essential activities only and going outdoors for exercise was considered an essential activity. If we complied with social distancing, we could pursue "walking, hiking, running or biking." We were allowed to go into public parks and outdoor recreation areas. The governor instructed us to avoid outdoor activities that "pose enhanced risks of injury or could otherwise stress local first responders to address the COVID-19 emergency, (e.g., backcountry skiing in a manner inconsistent with avalanche recommendations or in closed terrain." I appreciate his caution about avalanches and his good work.

No one knows what will happen next. States, cities, and towns are opening up. Montana is letting people go out, get haircuts, and be together in small groups. The two-week quarantine for everyone coming into the state has ended. Tourists are starting to come back and businesses are opening. In a few days Montana will open its three gates into Yellowstone National Park. I'm thankful to be here.

June 6, 2020: A lot has happened and a lot has changed since Memorial Day. On May 25, a black man named George Floyd was killed by Derek Chauvin, a white Minneapolis police officer, who knelt on his neck for more than eight minutes until he died. The horrific killing was captured on video and viewed by people around the world. Since then, there have been protests against police violence and racial injustice for 12 days and nights around the U.S. and the world. Bozeman has had two peaceful protests. Both had an impressive turn out: 2,000 people at the first rally and 3,000 at the second. These have to be the largest protests ever in our city. People want change and a strong turn toward fairness, decency, and justice. It feels like a historic turning point for America: turning away from the ugly, systemic, and violent racism of the past and toward a future where all Americans can breathe, thrive, and prosper.

There are immediate signs of change: the Minneapolis City Council voted to dismantle their police department and create a new system for public safety; the president ordered withdrawal of National Guard troops from the capital after strong criticism from the military establishment for using force against protesters in the capital and for threatening to send U.S. troops to other cities; the NFL's Commissioner admits "we were wrong for not listening to NFL players earlier" (but alas he does not speak about Colin Kaepernick). It will take a while before we know how far these and other immediate responses to the protests will grow and spread.

There is a recent ABC News poll that found 74% of Americans view the death of George Floyd as a sign of an underlying racial problem and not as an isolated incident. This is an increase of 30 percentage points since a similar poll was taken in 2014 after the shooting of Michael Brown and the death of Eric Garner, both black men killed by white officers. The survey results point to change in public opinion and an awakening of consciousness. More people realize police violence is not a matter of a few bad apples, but has deeper older roots that permeate every area of American life.

The Reverend Al Sharpton gave the eulogy for George Floyd and talked about the deep roots of racism: "When I stood at that spot [where George Floyd died], the reason it got to me is that George Floyd's story has been the story of black folks. Because ever since 401 years ago, the reason we could never be who we wanted and dreamed of being is you kept your knee on our neck. What happened to Floyd happens every day in this country, in education, in health services, and in every area of American life. It's time to stand up in George's name and say get your knee off our necks!" -Amen-

My favorite visual image representing hope for the justice revolution comes from Muriel Bowser, the mayor of Washington DC, who renamed an area in front of Lafayette Square "Black Lives Matter Plaza." She had city workers paint the words "Black Lives Matter" in gigantic bright-yellow capital letters covering the street. I imagine you could read those words from space.

One morning, I went out early and drove about an hour toward a favorite birding reservoir. On the way I spotted a commotion out of the corner of my eye. I stopped the car, but it was hard to see what was going on. I drove past the nest, turned the car around and went back to get a better view. An adult Bald Eagle was standing on the edge of the nest and I could see a little bit of another bird in the nest. I got a good view through the leaves with my binoculars and I could just see the head of the standing bird bent down over the nest. I could see the impressive beak opening and I could see the sharp hook at the end of the beak. There was a lot of foliage all around the nest and it was hard to see but it looked like the eagle put food in another mouth. As I drove away another adult eagle flew past headed in the direction of the nest. A week later, I went back to see what was happening at the nest. There were four birds, two adults perched in the tree close to the nest and two very large chicks standing up in the nest.

I thought seeing the eagle family with two adult eagles and two chicks was a good omen. With all that is going on, I look out for hopeful signs. Perhaps there was even a message from our powerful and beautiful national bird with its gleaming white head and tail: Work together, love each other, and take care of the planet we share.

Life in the Time of COVID-19
by Marcia Prather

Born in 1949 in Missoula, Montana,
Marcia Prather is a retired Family Medicine
and Emergency Medicine Physician
and lives in Florence, Montana.

The days all run together. No events differentiate the days: no exercise classes, no gatherings with friends, no church meetings or services, no medical appointments, no in-home tutoring sessions, no book club meetings, no dinners out. Tomorrow will look like today, which looks like yesterday.

I am fortunate that my shelter-in-place is happening at a time in my life when I don't have to go to work in a place. I can get outside and take long walks or sit on my deck and enjoy the sunshine. This pandemic seems urgently close and somewhat distant at the same time.

Though I obsessively watch the news, to the point that I think I have developed a TV crush on CNN's medical correspondent, Dr. Sanjay Gupta, I didn't think I was stressed by the pandemic until I developed the second cold sore of my life. But there it was: palpable, visible, and an indisputable sign of stress.

From the standpoint of a retired ER doctor, I find this time fascinating. I compulsively follow the reports about the possible origins of the virus, the epidemiology of its spread, the evolving recommendations for the prevention or mitigation of its further spread, the assessments of risk factors and the medical profiles of the casualties, the crisis over PPE (personal protective equipment), and the political conflict that has erupted over COVID-19 deaths versus an economic crisis.

How do we value a human life? Why does it seem that some lives are viewed as disposable? The wide gap between the haves and the have-nots has been made even more obvious during this pandemic. The relief I feel because I am living in a relatively safe place is in conflict with the angst I feel for those who are not, and with the anger I feel toward the politicians who so easily dismiss such a large portion of our society. These politicians not only blatantly lie to us, but see the economy as more important than people.

From the standpoint of an over 70-year-old woman with hypertension and severe underlying asthma and living with someone who is still required, as an essential worker, to go to work in his job as a psychiatrist with the Veterans Administration (though currently most of the patient interactions have gone to telemedicine), I find this time terrifying. I think about doctors having to make life-and-death triage decisions about who gets a ventilator and realize that in such a scenario, I might not qualify.

I read and hear about the front-line workers. I have friends and former colleagues there. I can imagine it, but at the same time it seems somewhat unreal. My state, Montana, has one of the lowest totals of cases and of deaths. My county has had only five documented cases, all travel related. I live in a poor area in a poor state, and here, people seem more concerned about the state of the economy than they do about the risk of illness and the loss of life. When I see someone out and about without a mask, I am angry that they value their personal comfort (or their political beliefs) more than my personal safety, or the safety of others. I am amazed that people do not realize that this virus does not have any political affiliation. It just wants hosts so it can replicate itself. For local people, death from COVID-19 seems remote, but the loss of livelihood seems imminent. Most people here know someone who has been severely affected economically. People living paycheck to paycheck are at risk of losing their incomes and homes and businesses. They fear they are losing not only their present but also their future. Many are clamoring to "open up" the economy. I think it will take local deaths for people to begin to understand the risks of this disease. I fear we as a society have lost the ability to empathize much beyond our immediate circumstances. I am bracing myself for a second, even more devastating, wave of infections.

I will continue to stay mostly sequestered. I will continue to binge-watch Netflix. I will continue to be grateful for digital technology that allows me to stay in contact with family and friends. I will continue to whittle away at the stack of books given and loaned to me by friends with the words, "You have to read this." My dogs and I will continue to do long walks in the fresh air, a luxury not available to so many. Perhaps I will perfect Instant Pot pinto beans. Maybe I will even get into the second layer of my ranch-girl overstocked freezer.

People talk about "the new norm" and what it might look like. My fear is that we won't make any changes and the new norm will look just like the old new norm. Well, maybe everyone will wash their hands more! I am grateful to be old, to have had a life where hugs weren't dangerous and if one socially distanced, it was by choice and not a choice of life or death.

The Fall
by Jane Quinn

Born in 1943 in Audubon, Iowa, Jane Quinn
is a retired owner of Quilting in the Country, now volunteers
at the city library and county historical museum
and lives in Bozeman, Montana.

Before COVID-19, and at 77 years old, I have enjoyed much of life. Not a day goes by that I don't experience memorable moments. My husband Bill and I are recent retirees and one of the benefits of retirement is allowing each day to simply unfold and embrace what happens. This global pandemic didn't radically alter how we already live our lives, but we will be certain to hug friends and family extra tight when we are out of this time. In fact, as farm kids, we take comfort in the change of seasons and new life in the spring. At the time, we have three new lambs running wild on our farmstead!

For me, what is most special about these unprecedented times is how they intersect with quiltmaking. My grandmother, also a craftswoman, loved to brush my hair and read to me. I can still remember the comfort of sitting on her lap while she read to me. Her lap was somewhat akin to being plunked down in a feather pillow; soft and cushy. We humans are social beings and connection is crucial. I have more time to reflect now, and I hope this new phase includes returning to more intimate times, like in the early days of spending time at Quilting in the Country. Maybe more patterns and books are in my future.

I do worry about all the people without someone to quarantine with, or the women and children in abusive relationships with no other option but to stay home with their abusers, along with the strain this puts on all areas of our country and the world. I also worry we are not done with this virus that had the capacity to close down the world as we know it, but is undetectable to the human eye.

When will schools, restaurants, and churches reopen and how does that look post-quarantine?

I pray for a vaccine and thank all of the front line workers who are working to make our lives as seamless as possible, while at great personal risk to themselves and their loved ones. Please thank them!

I'll close with a passage that I have always loved. It is from Leo Buscaglia's *The Fall of Freddie the Leaf* and is quite appropriate for this moment in time.

> "Then what has been the reason for all of this?"
> Freddie continued to question. "Why were we here
>   at all if we only have to fall and die?"
> Daniel answered in his matter-of-fact-way,
>   "It's been about the sun and the moon.
>   It's been about happy times together.
>   It's been about the shade and the old people
>   and the children. It's been about colors
>   in the Fall. It's been about seasons.
>   Isn't that enough?"

The Larger Picture
by Marcia Rueter Leritz

Born in 1944 in Wauneta, Nebraska,
Marcia Rueter Leritz is a retired graphic designer
and lives in Bozeman, Montana.

I've always been somewhat of a worrier, but that has been multiplied now with concern for my husband, sons, grandchildren, and friends who are now thrust into this mix of misinformation, incapable leaders, and a virus that seemingly respects no age or vulnerability. Yet, there is a calmness and serenity of this state; like floating underwater. Why do I find this vacation from washing sheets and last-minute Costco runs cathartic? Popcorn for dinner and pie for breakfast. Day pajamas and night pajamas. Sheer escape from most responsibility.

Years ago when I was cleaning the house for anticipated guests, my son who was 10-years-old at the time told me, "You adults do so many unnecessary things." He was right; I try to remember placing things into two columns: Necessary and Unnecessary. But now in our struggle to stay healthy, not only from the COVID-19, but our aging bodies, the columns have been upgraded: Life and Death.

"We're all in this together" is like a broken record coming at us from every newscast, discussion, and street corner. In actuality, we are not all in this together, we are not dealing with similar circumstances. People are dying, suffering financially, and risking their own health to work. While my life has changed very little since the onset of this pandemic,

I grieve for the homeless, the hungry, the refugees and immigrants, and the victims who take little comfort in that trite phrase.

The pandemic has pulled some families closer and broken others, but on the bright side, the natural world just might benefit from the slow down. Our government has stepped up with financial aid. Funny how some of the *wild* ideas like universal income and health care for all are gaining traction.

But the larger picture is, humans are disrupting ecosystems that have naturally regulated diseases and protected human health. By destroying and encroaching on vital habitats, we're breaking the barriers between humans and disease-carrying animals. An estimated three-fourths of all new infectious diseases originate in animals, and they almost universally emerge as a result of ecological disruptions. Biodiverse forests act as "reservoirs" where viruses, bacteria, and other microorganisms naturally live and grow. As we fragment their habitat with human activity, we break the reservoir and the diseases flow out, jumping the species boundary and entering human hosts. As species in the natural world disappear, viruses look for more population density in which to reproduce. With no evolved immunity, the rapidly reproducing humans spread those diseases.

We need to move away from the extractive capitalism that disrespects the natural world. We also must reimagine our place, understanding that as humans, we are not detached from the greater web of life. We, and the ecosystems of which we're a part, are deeply interdependent.

For many of us, this pandemic is a wake-up call. It's time to overhaul our current systems of extraction, exploitation, and destruction of our planet, individually and collectively, even if it involves self-sacrifice and wanting and living with less. What other choice do we have?

This shared calamity makes us more urgently alive, less attached to the small things, and more committed to the big ones. We have withdrawn from each other to protect each other. I can't even wonder how long this will take. All I know is that each one of you are still out there, responding, willing to help each other, and for today, that is enough.

> *"Let us love this distance, which is friendship,*
> *since those who love separated."*
> —Simone Weill

Wending Our Way
by June Billings Safford

Born in 1938 in Brooklyn, New York,
June Billings Safford is a retired teacher
and lives in Bozeman, Montana.

In early March, as the news of the COVID-19 pandemic was hitting the states hard, our daughter-in-law Kelly called to say her two sons, Marcel and Daniel, our grandsons, both in their 20s, had come down with the mosquito-borne virus, Dengue fever. They were at the beginning of a gap year in South East Asia. They were staying in a youth hostel on the main island of Indonesia. Kelly explained how sick they were: sudden high fevers, muscle aches, vomiting. It seemed so chronic that we all feared for their lives. The younger one's prognosis came from a clinic in a remote area which left us wondering if they might have the Corona virus, and Dengue fever. It became clear to us that they needed to be home, but news about plane flights being canceled and fewer and fewer passengers being allowed to board increased our anxiety. This unfolding drama served to unsettle me from the very beginning of this journey. I felt frantic. Thankfully, Marcel and Daniel made it home from their journey safely, but they, I, and the whole world embarked on a perilous journey not of our choosing.

I am nevertheless totally engaged in one occupation, that of caregiver for my husband Jeff of more than 60 years who suffers from Parkinson's Disease. I am past the age of employment, a retiree with time seemingly at my disposal. Before the stay-at-home policy, I did have the benefit of home health from First Choice for a few hours two days a week. Concerns about the virus led me to cancel such visits. Three of our four children live on opposite coasts and would not be able to fly. Our son who lives south of Buffalo, New York had already stayed with us for more than a month before news of the pandemic. Our younger daughter, Brooke lives closer, in Durango, Colorado and thought she might be available and could drive, but when she factored in that her partner is an ER doctor in a hospital that serves an Indian Reservation, that likelihood went by the wayside. In the middle of a phone conversation, Brooke began sobbing, expressing her fears for us: "We may never see each other again." This touched me deeply; I held the phone embarrassed because my thoughts had never ventured there.

The following day, I let myself think about who would care for Jeff if I contracted it. This thought that weighed so heavily on Brooke became mine and my tears flowed.

Living in Montana has been advantageous. Our numbers look low, even if they are not. I determine to stay informed and read *The New York Times*, *The Washington Post*, watch PBS and MSNBC. Our children caution us to stay positive and avoid being bad news junkies. Jeff exhibits little interest, or fear; it doesn't mean he doesn't know what's happening, just that he lacks any urge to share, to converse. This has meant we have very little conversation about what is going on in the world, which, I find, leads to an uncomfortable aloneness. I need to look for ways to reach out, especially since we have been the recipients of so much caring from our children, friends and neighbors. For example, for Easter, a couple delivered a roast lamb dinner. Our doorbell and our phone keeps ringing with offers of assistance. Love persists.

I find myself tuning in online to Bozeman Arts-Live! Concerts galore from local musicians, offering a chance for the viewer to leave a tip. Musicians are hurting.

I was stirred to think about COVID-19's effects on visual artists as well, having to store paintings, instead of sell them. It occurred that since I have always wanted to own an Aaron Schuerr pastel, perhaps this was the time to do just that. Now, we have a remarkable pastel of a section of Lava Creek gracing our vestibule, and he has a sale that maybe made a difference.

Even more adventuresome and pleasurable for me has been order-ing lattes and crepes from a struggling cafe in Boston. The owner wor-ries about how to keep her business afloat and since I know and adore her, I order. Should I check the box that says Deliver, or the one that says Pick Up? I love the playfulness of it all.

So whether it be COVID-19 or Parkinson's, I'm compelled to tap into the urge to keep us sane by tapping into my love of innovation. For supper last night, we ate a bowl of crab and corn chowder, and to make our experience more in-tune with New England, I moved a lobster buoy from the mantelpiece to the dining room table as a centerpiece.

At Wagner College, during his undergraduate years Jeff majored in piano. Now the black and white keys frustrate him, rather than bring him pleasure, but by limiting our musical choices to hymns from our Lutheran hymnal, he can still play the right hand, and we can sing together.

Breakfasts pose a challenge which I meet by topping our cereal with a dollop of Swedish lingonberries. If I really want to ratchet up the morning, I announce it's Dutch Baby time. The recipe comes right from a page of the *Bozeman Daily Chronicle*. It is an oven baked pancake, sprinkled with powdered sugar, strewn with fresh strawberries, or blue-berries. The addition of squeezed lemon juice on top of everything sweet makes this breakfast scintillating. In truth, Jeff has lost his sense of taste, a dictate of his syndrome, but the dish offers the up-lifting look of summer during March and April's remnants of winter.

Not by choice, Jeff and I live out our days in incremental fashion. First and foremost is making sure Jeff has opportunities to exercise, to keep his legs from entirely losing their mobility. The disease can wreak havoc on his efforts to stay balanced and avoid falls. Walking and exer-cise is what keeps him upright. Atrophy looms, unless. Physical therapy plays no small role in this endeavor.

We have found a way to escape the confines of home by fleeing to the sanctuary of our empty church. When Montana weather doesn't allow for outdoor walks, the staff has given Jeff permission to exercise with his walker, ranging out into the many areas of this expansive building. I appreciate being enveloped by the beauty and quiet of the sanctuary, to ponder what we both are experiencing. Out there, what surrounds us seems menacing so I pray for courage and strength to wrestle with what we have not chosen: advancing age, illness, a world-wide pandemic, isolation. The reality of no firm-footing still requires I put one foot in front of one another, while enduring and embracing what is. No matter what, even with my energy waning, these are times that still call forth whatever innovative spirit I can find.

A Scream Within A Scream
by Kelly L. Simmons

Born in 1961 in Salt Lake City,
Kelly L. Simmons is a writer
and lives in Bozeman, Montana.

I am a writer, so most days I sit inside in front of my computer. I still drink red wine at night and obsess over my work, I still read hours each day. I worry. It's much the same. And yet, I feel a marked difference.

I am more tense, I am quicker to criticize, to snap. I feel cagey, 'caught.' Why? I wonder.

I can still get out for long walks and drives. I've talked to more family and friends than I have in a long time. I take calls I wouldn't normally take, because, well . . . I should. And, mostly, because I want to, but throughout the 'normalcy' of my day, something feels off. The weight is heavy. More of a slog as I lift my tired feet on my long walks. Sometimes I want to scream. Sometimes I want to cry. Sometimes both, and at the same time. Again, I ask myself *why?* Because it's inescapable, that's why. The tug between connection and a disconnection. A connection by being human, and a disconnection of being cut off. Cut off both in experiences and literally.

And it's the numbers. The number of infections. The number of deaths. The number of women who will be abused, and more often. The number of children who will be neglected and mistreated. The number who will go hungry because they are not in school. The number of parents worrying right now about food and shelter. The number of us who look for some leadership and find none. The number of those who will find hate instead of love, fear instead of hope. Every day and night the newscasts beat with more of these numbers.

Yesterday, while driving, a motorcycle blasted past our car. We made the comment that he must have a death wish. And then a mere second later—the *CRASH*.

The cyclist blew through the red light, smashing into another cyclist. He flew off his bike, this young man, jumping up in an adrenalin rush, just as his ankle collapsed beneath him. He looked down, his pant leg loose and empty. The horror of recognition. The other cyclist did not get up. I didn't see the rest. The blood. The regret. The loss. The meaning of a single second and a stupid, stupid decision. We pulled over to call 9-1-1 as the experience settled over us. Became part of us forever. Another horror twisted into the pandemic.

A scream within a scream.

I suppose some would say one's perspective changes here. That's always seemed an inane remark to me: "*Sure changes your perspective on things.*" It makes me mad when I hear it. Not because it shouldn't change your perspective. It should. It's because the words feel ephemeral, fleeting. We will forget almost as soon as we learn it. But, I suppose, it's impossible to hold onto these opposing thoughts forever. Loving because of the possibility of loss. Why not loving because we love?

And the young man on the motorcycle? If he makes it. If his victim recovers? Will his perspective be changed forever? Perhaps. Perhaps it will. And for us? Will we remember?

I recall the first days after 9/11. The world seemed changed. Uplifted. We smiled at one another no matter our political affiliation. We felt connected. Can we strive for that on a world wide basis? Or will we retreat into our fear?

After witnessing the accident, I smudged our car, our house, my shoes, my feet, my heart. I have prayed for the victims. For they are all victims. I have cried. I have beat my chest for understanding. We are forever linked with tragedies, just as we are linked with joys.

I have a sense our human cup is full. And then I see the compassion that keeps on coming and making room. The millions of kindnesses. The reach of a hand even if it is virtual. And just as my bitter heart tightens with fear, it also floods with love. It is the human heart. And I am humbled. I am broken, but I am also renewed.

If we shut it off. Just shut it off. We can hear it. Just there. The nightly Bozeman howl, the cheers as a patient leaves the hospital, the gasp of recognition on the phone when we connect. The indomitable human spirit.

Chords of Memory
by Beth Sirr

Born in Colorado, Beth Sirr
is a Family Nurse Practitioner
and lives in Bozeman, Montana.

I am 61 years old, a mother, wife, and nurse. I am thinking about the essence and extreme beauty of nature: the sky, trees, birds, creeks, the essential world. I am grateful for this wildness in my life, more so as I think of all those confined to urban apartments or hospitals due to the coronavirus pandemic. I wonder a lot, too, about the human species, our faults, how we think and make decisions individually and collectively.

What shapes our understanding of each other and the world around us? What motivates us to respond with kindness vs cruelty? What pushes a society to cheer Hitler vs Gandhi? To emulate the Kochs vs Thoreau? How do ordinary individuals make a difference?

Once, I heard the Dalai Lama describe empathy as a natural sense, but one that humans needed to cultivate through the practice of kindness and compassion.

History provides countless examples of selfless heroism, creativity, and generosity that have made a positive difference for others, most notably, when confronting the opposite quality. Amid the horrors of Nazi death camps, both Dr. Viktor Frankl and Captain Witold Pilecki wrote about trees, birdsong, the hope of seeing loved ones and of how doing something meaningful for others helped sustain them.

How does a species capable of moral insight, also act so cruelly? How do the brains that believe in "Christianity," the "Golden Rule," and "the greatest of these is love," create death camps, or separate children from their asylum-seeking parents and lock them all up? How could the SS soldier who generously treated young Daniel Kahneman with the affection he had his own son, also act to kill him, if he discovered that Daniel was Jewish? How do the neurological circuits develop to believe and applaud men like Hitler, Mussolini, Stalin, Trump? Is it the need for a "savior"? Would these same people have followed Gandhi, MLK, Jesus?

Moral decision-making research suggests being in physical proximity, or having a personal relationship with someone, makes a difference when deciding to save nine people or one person. Our brains favor saving one person in proximity over nine people at a distance. Elected officials also act to help those they know vs the many they don't know: The consequences are considerable for the anonymous millions they don't know.

Neuro-wiring evolved to default, to favor those we are close to. This makes sense. Our survival is better ensured when we help our family, friends, and fellow villagers. However, on a planet with nearly 8 billion people, it has meant those in power are far removed from 99% of us. Our economic and political systems have devolved to serve the one, not the many.

As a nurse, I saw the disastrous consequences for patients when decisions were not made by those caring for them, by those seeing their faces and their suffering, but rather when the decisions were made by administrators and politicians far removed from the humans suffering.

The moral decision-making research explains how the problems that harm so many from poverty, war, gun violence, deforestation, climate change, the prison industrial system, to lack of affordable health care, shelter, healthy food and a quality education can be ignored by those in power.

Memories shared by my great aunt, Aunt Gilberte, made me want to make sense of our species and myself. When she was 17 years old, the Nazi's took over France and she began hiding Jews in her apartment. What would I do if I were in her shoes? She was later recruited by the Resistance and worked through the war transporting downed RAF pilots and Jews to safety. She witnessed and survived Nazi roundups and killing squads. What gave her the courage? She thought the decision came automatically in part because she grew up listening to WWI Veterans in her home. She always emphasized that her role in service was "small, many people did much more." In addition, she voiced a deep understanding for those who chose to protect their families and avoid danger for themselves reflecting on the absurdity of an ordinary person challenging the Nazi forces engaged in public brutality, armed with machine guns and tanks.

She chose to risk her life to do what she believed was right, and because of this I was so drawn to her. Her moral decision making wasn't a grand plan, it was basic: how can I help this person?

The foundations of moral decision-making had been so much a part of her upbringing that helping others was a natural, automatic response, with and without the Nazis. Acting heroically, on automatic, has been commonly reported in many first person accounts in other situations. How do we create and cultivate our better, kinder, heroic natures to be automatic?

Since 1979 , I've been a nurse. Nursing allows intimacy with strangers during times they are vulnerable, scared, suffering, and dying. Over the years, I've learned a beautiful truth: the energy to care for others is fueled by caring for others. Simply: the desire to help, the drive to care, ignites a force that steers the ability to work and care.

When you are sick, kindness matters most. Compassion, patience, science, simple acts that comfort all, can ease suffering and fear. COVID-19 has been an opportunity to nurture and practice kindness, compassion, and patience in our lives. As it has slowed down our species, made us more aware of a larger humanity, highlighted our vulnerability, will it also reorient our moral compasses? I hope so, but I worry, and therefore lean on these quotes, which seem appropriate:

> *"My religion is very simple. My religion is kindness."*
> —Dalai Lama

> *"The more clearly we can focus our attention on the wonders and realities of the universe about us, the less taste we shall have for destruction."*
> —Rachel Carson

*"For if we should perish, the ruthlessness of the foe would be only
the secondary cause of the disaster. The primary cause would be that
the strength of a giant nation was directed by eyes too blind to see
all the hazards of the struggle; and the blindness would be induced not
by some accident of nature or history, but by hatred and vainglory."*
—Reinhold Niebuhr, *The Irony of American History*, 1952

Stay Calm and Jesus On
by Nancy Slabaugh Hart

Born in 1955 in Caldwell, Idaho,
Nancy Slabaugh Hart is a United Methodist pastor
and lives in Madras, Oregon.

On Friday afternoon, March 13, 2020, I opened an email from Bishop Stanovsky, and everything changed. I was relieved . . . briefly.

For weeks prior, the stories of a possible pandemic had held the attention of the world. By March, it was clear that we were in a global crisis with COVID-19.

At first, it seemed as though we could keep everyone safe by simply using common sense precautions, like wash your hands, don't touch your face, reduce exposure by limiting travel. In church service, we stopped shaking hands during the *Passing of the Peace* and demonstrated proper hand-washing during announcements. I tried to model a non-anxious presence to reassure the congregation that we would find our way through this. Stay Calm and Jesus On.

Initially, the virologists, scientists, and medical experts seemed to have little to tell us except for the velocity with which the disease was spreading across the planet leaving devastation in its wake. Vulnerable populations were urged to take special care: the elderly; those with underlying health issues; those with respiratory ailments such as asthma and COPD. Those criteria could apply to most of the folks in my congregation, including me. This description covered nearly everyone we served through our various Food Ministries.

By the time the World Health Organization began to advise that large groups should not gather, I began to receive phone calls and emails from people in the congregation letting me know they would not be coming to church until the crisis was over. Some had already decided to shelter in place. Early in the "Week-When-Everything-Changed," I kept thinking: "Is it possible that we are over-reacting here?" By the end of the week, I had no idea which course of action made sense, I was completely torn: Open? Close? Open? Close?

Then it was Friday with the email from the Bishop. *All local churches of the Greater Northwest Area of the United Methodist Church shall remain closed until we are confident that, in the words of founder John Wesley, we will "Do No Harm."* This directive included all UM churches in Oregon, Washington, Alaska, and Idaho. All of us. And no pastor would have to make an impossible choice. It felt like a weight was lifted off my shoulders: I did not have to make the decision.

For a moment, I felt uplifted onto a wave of calm. The decision was made. No more ambiguity. It lasted about ten minutes. I miss that ten minutes.

After the calm, came the questions. At 65 years old, I am barely eligible to consider myself an "elder" but I felt very old. I was part of a vulnerable population, trying to lead a vulnerable population—to keep my people safe, and still, provide for the more vulnerable people in our community. A quick check-in with some of my younger colleagues found them poised to shift quickly. Many churches were already providing live-streaming services to their congregations. The only immediate change for them would be the audience. Everyone would be watching from home. Those who were not already providing online worship were looking at a variety of platforms: Facebook Live, Zoom, and some had hit on the notion of connecting via FM radio and listening in to the service in cars parked, like a Drive-in theater, in their church parking lots. And then there were the equipment conversations—clergy were posting their home studio pictures—some of which looked like they were preparing either for Armageddon or an at home version of Masterpiece Theater.

My age was against me. I had "views" about what could and should be done, but absolutely no expertise, or what younger generations call *tech savvy.*

Having followed a number of churches experimenting with live-streaming, I was skeptical. There were so many things that could go wrong, particularly if you didn't have staff, or strong volunteers, who knew what they were doing. Being the "staff" in charge, it was overwhelming, and a blow to my natural competitive streak. (Not very humble of me, I realize, but I am human.) I knew enough to be aware that there were issues like streaming speed, lighting, staging, and sound quality that could make or break a good outcome.

According to the professional literature I have read, seminars I have attended, and professional coaches who have guided me in the last 20 plus years, the "most essential quality of an effective pastor in the 21st century" is adaptive leadership. And I believe it is true. I have always tried to be *adaptive* and resilient. But, in such a time as this, I began to wonder—am I too old for this shit? (Did I say that out loud ?)

In ancient times, the People of God were displaced by what biblical scholars refer to as the Babylonian Exile. Everything they knew about themselves centered around the Land and the Temple. When they had neither, they had questions, like: is God still with us, if the "house" of God is gone? Are we still God's people, when we are not able to be in the correct location? How do we worship, if we can't do things the way we have always done them?

This parallel didn't come to me until later, but the aptness of the comparison continues to prove valuable insight. In the early years of the 21st century, the church found itself at a crossroads. The culture was going through dramatic changes—in values, in the speed of new information, in technology. The Church and her Leaders asked: What does it mean to "be church" in this time? Are we willing to *be church* in a different way? What are we willing to let go of, if we want to bring faith to generations who have disconnected with the church and with new generations of folks who have never been connected? COVID-19 has pushed us in the direction of creativity and resilience. Who are we when we cannot be where and what we were before? We must adapt or disappear, while at the same time holding to our most central core values, lest we become just one more consumable commodity.

On that first Friday night, my husband thoughtfully poured me a glass of wine as I collapsed into my comfy recliner, and after a couple of restorative sips, I called my son. My first question was: "What is the *very easiest* way for me to bring worship to my congregation on Sunday?" We discussed the various options, and then decided I would pre-record. Low-tech. Ability to edit. And, perhaps most important, the possibilities for "do-overs."

Early Saturday morning, I recorded a sermon in my office. We propped up my iPhone against a pile of books and hymnals on a rolling stand in front of my desk, as I sat trying to look comfortable in my office chair. My husband gently turned on the record button, sat down in his chair, and coughed. I glared at him, and we started again. The second time through, the custodian walked by my office pushing a squeaky cart. We started again. Each time we started again, I felt more anxious. I can't remember how many times we restarted that video, but it was hands down one of the most anxiety-provoking things I have ever had to do as a public speaker.

Preaching, for me, is a kind of mystical process. It is hard to describe, except that being in the midst of the congregation is every bit as important to me as the content I prepare. I don't refer to notes, I use people's faces and body language to find my place (literally and metaphorically.) It is a conversation—between me, the people and God. It is prayer. And I love it. This new thing was awkward. And weird. And my hands shook.

My son Jonathan, who is wise in the ways of technology, expressed concern that I might make myself ill due to the amount of anxiety I seemed to be experiencing (e.g. "You might be too old for this shit") and volunteered to take on the task of running it through his editing and rendering equipment from 100 miles away. It was a wonderful gift, but also bothersome, as we realized that the bandwidth and internet speed in a small Oregon town was much slower than he had available to him in Portland. It made sending him videos and slides very, very slow and tedious. To an already anxious preacher, this was downright painful. In spite of all the setbacks, Jonathan had everything ready by early Sunday morning. And, much to my amazement, people watched it. Even more shocking, my congregation, without any prompting, began to share the link with friends, relatives, and acquaintances. Within a couple of weeks, we were reaching more people electronically than we had been reaching in person: young people, old people, church people, no-longer church people. Friends. Strangers. Seekers. A totally unexpected outcome. We even had a former parishioner, who had relocated to Ecuador, who was an avid follower.

Every Friday became recording day. In theory, there was no one in the office on this day. This was not always the reality. Interruptions were frequent at first, and increased the stress upon my nerves, all out of proportion to said interruption. But we persevered. My tech staff (Jonathan) began to talk me through ways in which we could improve the recording. We began to add a few bits of equipment—a microphone, a tripod, and eventually, I even upgraded my phone. The "team" is currently in discussion regarding the addition of a green screen (my idea) and additional lighting (Jonathan's idea). I am learning. I am adapting. I am tired. The gift of this moment, however, is that I am beginning to understand that I don't have to be comfortable or swift or adept, in order to be adaptive. Perfect need not apply, but I confess, however, that as much as I am trying to give up on perfection, a part of me would still love to create a high-quality end product that might impress my younger colleagues. I do, as I have already admitted, have a bit of a competitive streak.

But mostly, I miss being with my folks. I want to return to the "room where it happens" soon. However, I am now in a much broader conversation than I could have imagined. I hear from people through comments, emails, texts, and even through a Zoom Bible Study. I would never have dreamed that this crisis would evolve into a new way to connect, to belong, to be in ministry.

On the first Monday morning AC, (After COVID), there were many more questions to unpack. What about our Food Ministries? What about the Blood Drive? What about AA? What about the groups that have already reserved the fellowship hall this month? Do we just shutter our doors and wait? Some pastors were still using their sanctuaries to stream, or record their worship videos, but many had chosen to leave the building completely, and set up shop online at home. As I scan the growing conversation strings on my social media clergy pages, I admit to feeling a bit wistful as I read of friends and acquaintances staying home—letting go of the pressures of meetings, schedules, and finding more time for reading and hobbies. As an introvert, this sounded perfectly delightful. (I could have a hobby!) I suspect not all was calm and bright, in the lives of all these clergy friends, but you couldn't tell that by following the conversation. I suppose we were all putting our best foot forward.

My congregation of just over 100 people has spent the last several years clarifying our values and purpose. We try to align everything we do through the lens of our mission, vision, and values. In its briefest form, it all comes down to these two things: We feed people: Body, Mind and Soul. And, All Are Welcome.

Feeding people in the time of the coronavirus pandemic was not just a value, but clearly an essential service. We didn't need to wring our hands about what our response to the changes happening in our state should or could be, we just needed a plan. We have had multiple food ministries over the years. The county in which we live is, according to the Health Department, one of the least healthy and resilient in the state, based on yearly statistical evaluations. Two programs, the Community Food Pantry and the Free Food Market provided patrons the opportunity to come into the building and do their own shopping.

The Food Ministry Director and I developed a work-around so that no one, but pantry volunteers would be allowed in the building. The two programs were collapsed into one, and we decided to launch a drive-up delivery service. Many folks in the community who under normal circumstances would not need a food pantry, were now in need of food. Part-time jobs, service jobs, and non-essential workers were laid off. The need was enormous. And, for the moment at least, there was no one else to whom they could turn.

Besides figuring out logistics, we immediately faced a volunteer shortage, like many other volunteer organizations, the viability of our all-volunteer organization depended heavily on retired people. Many of our most dedicated workers had underlying health issues that prevented them from continuing to help. Some workers were told by their adult children, in no uncertain terms, that they were to stay home. In spite of this, people stepped up. Again, many of those who came were retired, but they were determined. Some of those whose had stepped away initially, came back, feeling that they couldn't stay away. They were willing to take the risk of helping, because the value of the work was real. It wasn't some random busy work designed to fill empty days and get them out of the house. This was a necessary work that gave to the community and provided meaning and purpose to life. It was soul work. For me, one of the gifts of being an "older" pastor, is that the bumps and bruises of life have given me the temperament and skill to work well in a crisis. I can identify situations that may lead to conflict in people who are under stress, and I can diffuse emotional bumps in the road. I'm good at it, or as my son Devin says, "It was in my wheel-house." This part of the re-tooling was no piece of cake, but I didn't wonder if I was beyond my expiration date.

To say this was a labor-intensive enterprise is a gross understate-ment. For example, instead of volunteers driving to the neighboring city of Redmond to pick up food twice a month, it became clear we would need to do so weekly. Rather than picking up 6-8,000 pounds of food, we were now picking up 8-12,000 pounds. Compared to a year ago, we doubled the number of households who were being fed. We made many refinements in detail over the first few weeks—sanitation, distance, crowd control, packaging. For a couple of weeks, it was nearly impossible to obtain gloves, masks, and hand-sanitizer. The community stepped up, sewing masks, dropping by gloves, and checks to keep us going.

Before the advent of COVID-19, our society was already stressed and anxious. We worried about climate change, school shootings, immi-gration, the deep divisions in our society, increasing signs of racism, outside interference in elections, violence against women and children, sexual slavery, the list is nearly endless. As Brene Brown has said so well (long before the time of global pandemic), "Every morning we wake up to the news to find out what we are supposed to be afraid of today, and who is to blame." And it was true. So, where are we now?

It is worse. Much worse.

Speaking from my own experience, there are times when I will suddenly experience anxiety, when I can find no particular reason or cause—I am not obsessing or actively worrying—but the anxiety hits as if it were just one more symptom of the deadly global disease. My brain feels fuzzy, and it seems to take an inordinate amount of time to compose a sentence—spoken or written. Some things that I enjoy doing, I simply do not have the "bandwidth" to do. Creativity is harder. Energy is low. There are days when I feel as if I were moving about in a vat of Jell-O. (When I imagine this, the Jell-O is always red. I have no idea why, but definitely RED.)

There is a sense of loss and grief. Shortly before the pandemic took over our lives, my mother died. I was able to be with her at her death. I was grateful. Now I am grateful that she died in February. If she had died after March 15, I would not have been able to be with her.

Now, we cannot be with our loved ones when they die, or when they give birth, or when they are in the hospital. We cannot be there for graduations, birthday parties, or even to just touch base. I miss my peeps. I want to hold them. I want to sit close. I want to go to the beach! It is a loss. I feel it. And there are days when I am sad.

Other people are angry. And I understand. But it makes me fear for the safety of my family, medical health workers, grocery store employees, emergency responders, even our Food Pantry volunteers and church staff. Anxious people do scary things.

But here is what I know. I knew this before, but I think I know it on a different level these days: we are all essential. We are all necessary. Our universe is connected in such a way that we are inextricably linked and interdependent. Old people. Young people. Clever. Silly. Obstinate. Different colors, ethnicities, shapes, orientation, religious, non-religious, the weakest and the strongest. My well-being and your well-being are tied. We need the earth, the earth needs us. We are in this together. Age can bring wisdom. Or, it may not, but perhaps, just perhaps, a crisis may bring with it an opportunity to re-set and re-tool, to make a fresh start, adapt to hard things, develop resilience, and create a new normal—no matter how close or how far we are to our expiration date. And I am blessed.

Pioneers
by Kathy Springmeyer

Born in 1955 in Hot Springs, Montana,
Kathy Springmeyer is a Director of Publications
and lives in Helena, Montana.

My favorite bedtime stories were from my father. He told me about growing up in a small town in North Dakota during the Great Depression, and about his mother struggling to raise eight kids as a single parent. She took in boarders and cooked, washed laundry, and sewed. Anything to make ends meet.

Dad told me about going down to their cellar one time to find potatoes for dinner. He found only one potato left to share between the nine of them. He also talked about the locusts darkening the sky as if it were night, then eating all the crops, along with the wooden handles off of tools. He recalled the time a door-to-door comb salesman came to the door, and how he embarrassed his mother by showing the salesman the family's comb, which was missing many of its teeth!

My father said everyone experienced the same hardships then, so their situation seemed normal at the time. Still, he acknowledged my grandmother was probably at her wit's end. At times, all they had to sustain themselves with was their family's great love and respect for each other.

My father told me these stories with fondness, not sadness. I sat in awe as I listened, trying to fathom what it would be like to not have anything to eat, something I know many experience now. Lately I hear the words, "Stay safe." I wonder what people said then.

My mother was forty-seven years old when my father died. When she retired, she moved back to their beloved cabin on Dickey Lake in Trego, Montana. We had brief visits on and off over the years that were usually full of tasks she needed done to get her through the winter.

During one of the last 4th of July parties we had at her cabin, friends of hers said they worried that she was beginning to show signs of dementia. Over the next year it became apparent that she was becoming a danger to herself.

We managed to keep her home through most of that year with family members caring for her. I anxiously read anything I could to learn about Alzheimer's disease. We decided that the safest thing would be to move her to Helena, where my brother and I live.

Mom was always such an independent, strong woman. She loved that people called her a pioneer woman, and she certainly lived up to that title. She had lived alone for several decades in a rugged, remote part of Montana, but in Helena she finally began to relax and lean on us more. She said she finally retired at the age of 86, much to our amusement. During her year and a half in Helena, I spent more time with her than I ever had. We enjoyed our moments together.

Mom fell and broke her pelvis at the end of January. After that, she needed close supervision in order to be safe. We sat next to her all day, every day, to ensure she remembered to eat and drink, keep her from falling from her wheelchair, and laugh with her while she chortled with joy at seeing elephants or seals on the Nature Channel as if seeing them for the first time. We calmed her when she was upset and attended to her pain with the help of aides and nurses. We expected her to make it through this injury with the same grit and fortitude she had met so many other challenges with.

The physical therapy for her broken pelvis caused her intense pain, but the rehab staff encouraged her to keep going. Her motivation was difficult to maintain because she would forget why she was there. She had small victories, but eventually her body gave up and she went downhill very quickly. We moved her into hospice care for a few days before she died. My strong mother passed away quietly, and I found myself alone with her body while waiting for one of my out-of-town brothers to arrive. There was a calm. She was no longer in pain.

We planned her memorial for March 10. Around this time we started hearing about the corona virus creeping closer to Montana. It was uncertain if we could still have the memorial, but we continued to put plans together.

We had a nice, simple gathering celebrating her life. We decorated the room with fresh flowers, displayed paintings and quilts she had created over the years, and shared stories about her life. My family went home exhausted from the events of the last two months. We talked about going on vacation somewhere, but I didn't have the energy to plan a getaway. Our son was going to stay a few more days and then go back home.

A snowstorm hit that weekend, so he decided to stay and wait for the roads to clear. He started to feel sick with a sore throat. No fever or cough, the symptoms everyone warned about, so we weren't concerned. But he didn't feel well enough to make the trip home.

I felt like I was fighting his bug off at first. At some point, I noticed that my taste and smell were gone. A couple of weeks later, I was overcome with chills and a slight fever for about three hours, and then it passed. My husband, who had been suffering with mononucleosis since November, felt like it was returning with a vengeance.

His breathing became short and rapid, and he became exhausted and confused. When he said he felt like he was dying, we took him to the hospital's emergency room. We dropped him outside, where the nurses greeted us in their masks and other protective gear. He tested positive for COVID-19 the next day. We didn't see him except on the occasional video calls when he had the strength. As more information about the virus began dominating the news, my son and I were afraid. It became unclear whether or not my husband would win this battle. We celebrated the good moments when he seemed slightly better, and sobbed together when he seemed to falter.

While he was in the hospital, my son and I also tested positive for the virus. No more leaving our postage stamp sized property except for doctor's appointments and emergencies. Where did we catch this bug? We didn't know anyone who'd been infected. Had we been unsafe? After a week of ups and downs, my husband surprised us by saying he was being released from the hospital.

One night as I woke from a dream, I wondered if I might be able to start grieving my mother's loss now. I still have some of her woolen sweaters that she loved to wear. Seeing the edge of one of her favorites in a pile of dirty clothes, I felt her presence with me from my laundry room floor. She speaks to me still, that tough pioneer woman. She says: Be strong, stay safe.

During this time of chaos, loss, and love, my husband, son and I have been isolated at home. My son is looking forward to feeling strong and going back to his life. I continue to work from home. I feel thankful, as many have lost their jobs around the country. My husband is feeling better and better. His personality is coming back. His stories are getting longer—a good sign!

People continue to ask if we've recovered yet, and the answer is complex. There is an impatience to feel the effects of this virus behind us. But in small ways it continues to keep its hold: fatigue, slight tightness to the lungs, test results that fluctuate between positive and negative for weeks. But in the ways that matter, we've recovered: We're together again.

Lovely neighbors, friends and family dropped off meals, shopped for us, and walked my son's dog. We've been sustained by the kindness of others. All these years later, I can relate to my father's stories of surviving the Depression, and why compassion was so important then and now. I think of my mother, the pioneer woman, carrying firewood back into her cabin alone in the winter, and I realize there can be strength and reflection in isolation. The returning warmth of spring sunshine nourishes our souls and gives us a sense of well being and healing. We look forward to having our lives back and returning to some kind of normalcy. Be strong. Stay safe.

Corona Virus Spring
by Jo Anne Salisbury Troxel

Born in 1933 and a third generation Montanan,
Jo Anne Salisbury Troxel is a writer, poet, social activist,
arts advocate, and a retired English Teacher,
and lives in Bozeman, Montana.

My first day of quarantine, I went to the store and purchased staples, soap, the last bottle of Purell. People go by with a sense of purpose, a destiny they didn't plan, but are willing to embrace. The shelves are empty in many areas, and strangely threatening. The carts are high with toilet paper as well as sanitizers and a ready supply of water; staples like dried beans, pasta, oatmeal, rice, are new purchases in case shortages occur. One of the store managers tells me they have had their busiest day since Christmas. He is feeling happy and successful, even jubilant.

There's a fever in this, stoked by our fear of microbes taking over and resistant to anything we can do. We are in the midst of a human tragedy, our collective science fiction nightmare. At the same time, we believe we can follow the protocol and be safe: wear a mask, distance 6 feet apart, wash our hands, stay in place. The current president calls it a "Democratic Hoax," the same way he refers to the hoax of global warming. The coronavirus, he assures us, will just "disappear." Rather than uniting our country against the virus and finding a solution, he chooses to separate us. Why?

I feel the world watching us, waiting to see what the richest nation that ever was will do to lead the world against this malign force. Confusion and chaos reign. Our hospitals and first responders are overwhelmed with the sick and dying. There are not enough ventilators, swabs, PPE (Personal Protective Equipment). Because this virus is so virulent and has such a will to find a host and complete it's life cycle, people can be contagious but with no symptoms. Many of the affected die alone, with loved ones watching, weeping. There is no ordinary life to fall back on. We live in the surreal life of a pandemic, a silent, hidden enemy that springs to life by threatening ours. And the news is more dire every day. Germs are everywhere . . . door knobs, mail box, mail, the newspaper. I have not been in a store since March 12. Price Rite delivers my medication; Heebs delivers groceries.

Tomorrow is April first, and the quarantine is on for the whole month, and possibly May, too. Tonight, on the radio, I heard this pandemic may last two years. I will be 88 years old by then. Today, looking in the mirror, I thought I looked pale, tired. Being around people makes one feel more attractive, more energized. All the protocols of hand washing and mask wearing leave a somber, heavy weight. Numbers of deaths and suffering fill the void of the days as I watch the news. The virus, unseen, a molecule covered with a corona, is endlessly fascinating. How could such a small thing wreck our complacency, bring such havoc on a species that put a man on the moon?

The Senior Center, where MWF I did weight lifting has closed. The Unitarian church, my Sunday habit for over fifty years years, is curtailed now until May 2021. My book club, the Paper Dolls, is cancelled for April. We are all restless, use humor to cheer each other out of the doldrums. "All you need is a wardrobe of two pairs of pajamas: one for daytime, one for sleeping."

These past weeks, I have donned a mask, taken my dog McGee to the Gallagator trail. He wanders around the sodden grass, sniffing, being a happy dog. People I meet, walking their dogs, veer left or right to maintain their distance. We wave in a new spirit of camaraderie. The trees barren but with buds, all signs of spring, lift my spirits. Volatile Montana spring evenings, I dress warmly and walk the empty streets like a homeless person. It is quiet, serene. I see no one. The many shops on a busy street are shuttered. I revel in the freedom, even as I am often being pelted with a sharp wind and bites of snow. After such a walk,

I am happy to turn toward home, and look forward to reading, listening to music, calling a friend. I like to remember that Tokyo citizens, because of their sequester, after untold years see the miracle of blue skies. The now empty beaches in California have brought the dolphins back to cavort close to the shore.

My life is closing down more each day. I am grateful that Spring is unfolding, and the long days will be full of light. The pandemic rages. Today, the US has more cases than any other country in the world with 464,865 sick people; 16,498 have died. There are 16 million jobless claims. 799 died in NYC on Wednesday.

How poorly this mad, self-centered, president has dealt with this pandemic! He closed down testing labs and science research teams. *The Boston Globe* said of him, "Trump has blood on his hands . . ."

Spring Break nears and many students called it off if they were going with elderly parents, grandparents. The cruise my granddaughter Sarada and I had planned we cancelled because of the virus.

From Yale epidemiologist, Jonathon P. Smith, about social distancing, wearing a mask: "This enemy that we are facing is very good at what it does; we are not failing. We need everyone to hold the line as the epidemic inevitably gets worse."

This is my world now. At 86, I am committed to honoring the days of my life and the world I was born into. I have a childish wonder about the sky, the moon and stars. In the middle of the night, awakened by some strange dream, I venture out the front door, and stand on the boulevard and watch the trees against the night sky. Everything is mysterious, strange, and new . . . There is something changing, something waiting beyond this time, this pandemic. What will we imagine into existence? Will we listen to what the world is telling us, and respond, repent, and repair?

The other day, Taylor Benoit, who takes care of the yard, called across the fence to tell me he would clean my yard for free, just some way he could give back in this crises. He did a beautiful transition of dead leaves and mud into a welcoming courtyard. My daughter Alli put all the furniture back in place, and I stood in the middle of the sunny, groomed courtyard, and cried. There is this, the beauty, and there is the loneliness, the fear, and the suffering. Alli's consolation was simple but true: "There is a lot to cry about in this messed up world."

The Constitution, the separation of powers, means nothing to this president. We watch, astounded, but no one stops him. He willfully flaunts every law, every rule. Impeachment looms.

Senate Republicans, where are you?

I am taken back to my youth when I was fourteen years old. All the Arlee junior high and high school students took the bus to Missoula to see the Freedom Train. Our history teacher explained that it was an honor to be able to view these important documents, the foundation of our Democracy, signed into law by our forefathers, the founders of our nation. I learned that the Constitution, Bill of Rights, gives citizens the right to assemble, to protest. There was even a letter from Christopher Columbus. The purpose was educational, but also to instill patriotism.

The Heritage Foundation, sponsors of the train, mandated that all races were to mingle on the seven car train, or the train would not stop in that state. Two states refused to be on the train with African Americans: Memphis, Tennessee, and Birmingham, Alabama. The train, true to this edict, raced through those states.

Changes are happening, and I watch from afar the revolution of people protesting about police brutality concerning the death of George Floyd, and understand the term "systemic racism." So many black men have been killed by police. The protests go on for days. My friends and I have animated conversations. Is this a revolution paralleling this conservative administration? Are right-wing protesters causing the chaos in an otherwise peaceful protest? And the others . . . the careless opportunists that come out and cause chaos because they care about nothing . . . ?

At the same time, there are floods, hurricanes, and fires. The Pandemic is ever present; we now have more deaths than all countries put together. I think of the Yeats poem "The Second Coming" the prophetic lines:

> Turning and turning in the widening gyre
> The falcon cannot hear the falconer;
> Things fall apart; the center cannot hold;
> Mere anarchy is loosed upon the world,
> The blood-dimmed tide is loosed, and everywhere
> The ceremony of innocence is drowned;
> The best lack all conviction, while the worst
> Are full of passionate intensity.

There are many suggestions about how to spend this pause in our usual routine. Being self-reflective, we may emerge a different people, less materialistic, more in tune with others, protect nature with new insights as a legacy for our children.

We are certain of nothing. Sometimes, I think of those days when I so effortlessly met friends for coffee, went to the library, bookstores, plays, concerts; had folks in for dinner, where we talked about everything from current events to future possibilities, and spontaneous laughter created a sense of closeness and harmony. I miss the adventure of life itself, and close, warm, human contact. I want to hug my daughter. I want to hug my friends, laugh, and talk about this time in the past tense, and, just maybe, I'll be a part of a new world unfolding. That idea grounds me in hope.

Angst
by Mattie Whitehouse

Born in 1943 in Denver, Colorado, Mattie Whitehouse
is a retired Northwest Airlines Customer Service Agent
and Docent at the Museum of the Rockies
and lives in Bozeman, Montana.

Websters defines bruxism as the habit of unconsciously gritting or grinding the teeth especially in situations of stress or during sleep.

Bruxism, to me, says: "Pay attention to what I'm telling you." That's how it starts. We must pay attention to the signals our bodies send us, no matter how subtle they may seem. The first time it happened to me was in 2008 when my husband was very ill. Meditation and deep breathing helped; bruxism subsided.

Bruxism started again this February after hearing conflicting information coming from China, Italy, New York City and Washington D.C. This time, turning off the television helped, but still I woke up in the night with my teeth grinding, my jaw clenched, aching.

Bruxism. This has subsided remarkably, but could easily begin again.

I try to analyze the situation we are in. Not wanting to sound cavalier about the world pandemic, but I don't fear for myself. Yes, I will do all I can to prevent my falling ill, but I truly fear for my two daughters: one, a physician, the other, a Neonatal Intensive Care Unit (NICU) nurse, both working in the University of Minnesota Health Care System. I especially fear for my two grandsons, aged two. We seem to think we are unique, but this isn't the first time a pandemic has destroyed large swaths of the human population; we always bounce back, increasing the population each time. At last count, just shy of eight billion humans. This is how every virus, man-made or natural, thrives . . . large populations crammed together and our touchy-feely ways of socializing. The opportunistic virus has found the perfect host and it is thriving and multiplying.

We have suffered through television and radio ads spouting platitudes you might find in a high school yearbook. My favorite is "We are all in this together." Are we really all in this together? I think not. Our American privilege prevents us from seeing the world from another perspective. Our behavior has been classically selfish. Some Americans have found comfort in toilet paper, some in pasta, others in Clorox or bottled water. When we should be thinking of those less fortunate, we think of ourselves and hoard what brings us comfort. In this country, the golden rule has changed to: *Do it to others, before they do it to you.*

I fear for our country under the current leadership: a country divided racially, religiously, politically and economically, and if anything, I see the wedge being driven down further. This test is going to be the turning point for our country's survival, and that of democracy. In times of turmoil and crisis countries look towards their elected officials for information, guidance, strength, hope, a person who is capable of leading with compassion, truthfulness and grace.

We have a leader unlike any other. He is incapable of giving any of the aforementioned. He is a bully, a tyrant, and a rumormonger who repeatedly lies to the American public. He is incapable of telling you the correct time if he were looking at a clock. Unfortunately, his agenda has been clear from the beginning, undermine all that the previous administrations have built, do as little as possible for the general public, and reap as much wealth as possible for himself. Meanwhile, our standing in the eyes of the world is severely diminished, and we find that our educational system is inferior, and our health care is inadequate and inequitable.

Lastly, I fear for our earth and all our fellow travelers; they certainly don't deserve what we have done to them. Overuse of pesticides has poisoned their land and water; our fossil fuel use has poisoned their air and environs; our large carbon footprint is responsible for the extinction of flora and fauna alike, and we have put all life on earth on a path to extinction. Life has been on this planet for about 1.6 billion years and we all share the same common ancestor. We are not as special as we would like to believe, sharing 90% of our genes with the chimpanzee, 85% with the cow, 65% with the chicken, 47% with the fruit fly, and 24% with a grain of rice.

We have marched across the continents, destroying the environment and the earth's inhabitants as we go. The great ape with the big brain is not so powerful; he can be brought down by a microscopic virus. This is our chance to improve, and prove ourselves worthy of sharing this globe with our fellow travelers. In the past few months our air and water quality have improved and wild animals are trying to reclaim some of the territory we have stolen from them. Our Mother Earth wants to heal, and can, if given the chance; she is resilient. We are all in this together.

Thoughts on These Times
by Susan Wickland

Born in 1954 in Wisconsin,
Susan Wickland is a retired Physician
and lives in Montana.

I am terrified I may never get to hold my daughter again.

I've made promises in my life that I haven't kept. Promises to loved ones. Betrayals to friends. Intentional omissions that still haunt me. But right now, the promise I have made to myself and to my daughter, to stay safe, to stay away from people, to not risk in any way getting the Coronavirus disease, so that someday, the day she gives me the okay, I can drive without stopping the 760 miles to her home, park the car, run up the steps, and hold her. That promise I will not break.

Mostly, I don't mind being alone. Mostly, I prefer it. The stay-at-home order we are living in is not a huge hardship. Being a hunter and a gardener, accomplished in home canning and food dehydrating, I'm not afraid of not being able to feed myself, keep my house warm, or problem solve for basic needs. I am appalled at the selfish behavior of people protesting the stay-at-home orders. I watched the news with near disbelief, then horror and disgust, as white men armed with assault rifles stormed the Michigan State Capital in protest of the stay-at-home order put in place by Michigan Governor, Gretchen Whitmer. No one was arrested. Imagine, if you will, the same armed protest carried out by immigrants, or Blacks, or Native Americans. I like to imagine that a huge wheel represents our societal experience, but we have lost a cog, a piece of our humanity, and it may never be fixed.

I can be obsessed with things. It may be my way of coping when the world shifts. Most days, in this time of COVID-19, I listen to the news. Obsessively, listen to the news. Then, one day singer-songwriter John Prine died from COVID-19 and I turned off the news, and spent the next two days listening to his music. Listened to "Hello in There" over and over. I listened to more music in two days than I have listened to in the nine years since my first granddaughter died.

On Day 3, I sat out with my morning coffee and wrote down everything I could hear for an hour. Birds. A cacophony of birds. Sand Hill Cranes headed for the reservoir. Red Winged Blackbirds, like on the pond where I grew up. A Chickadee, which is the voice of my dead Grandmother. A Robin, Magpies, Bluebirds, Rosy Finches, Swallows, that Robin again, and finally a Meadowlark. Not a single voice, or engine, or plane. Not even a dog barking. That Robin again. I became obsessed with bird songs, especially the Robin. I wrote a brief letter, to go along with the list, and mailed it to my 7-year-old granddaughter, born just 15 months after the first granddaughter died, hoping, but not suggesting, she keep this letter and read it again as an adult, maybe remembering something about me.

The children. What will they remember? What will my granddaughter remember of the years before Coronavirus pandemic? Will my outgoing, playful, trusting granddaughter be able to run out her door to the neighbors, hugging everyone she knows on her city block, sharing the cookies she helped bake, finally landing at her friend Jack's house, where all the kids pile together on a couch to watch *Frozen II* again? Will she remember when that was all possible? Or will it be possible again? I don't believe it will, but it would crush her if someone told her that now.

I am a burned-out doctor, have given up my medical license, and never want to be responsible for some one else's life ever again. I say that, but right now, I am feeling guilty for not being in the hospitals or clinics, doing something, anything, to help in this COVID-19 crisis. But as much as the guilt, I feel paralyzed. The wrong advice, the wrong timing, the wrong instrument could cost a life. Has cost a life. My simple contribution right now is to sew masks. My god, it has come to this. We sew face masks. I finish another mask and cry. Again. I am scared.

My grandmother lived through the Spanish Flu, my father came home from WWII, my mother survived an abusive husband, regrouped when he died young, remarried, and started a domestic abuse shelter. I faced violent protesters, death threats, wore a bullet-proof vest and a concealed weapon because I choose to provide abortions. I survived invasive breast cancer. Those were limited events. My daughter and granddaughter will have to live the rest of their lives with some level of "social distancing" as the standard. My two-month-old great, great niece, born in this perilous time, will not be passed around a group of adoring elders wanting to kiss her cheeks. At the most critical time of their development, the time of learning how to trust themselves and the world, our babies and children are being taught not to touch, to hug, to trust. I am afraid of what these messages, this social distancing will do to their sense of being, their emotional development, their way of communicating for the rest of their lives. I'm old and have wonderful memories of greeting my neighbors with a hug, and right now, I ache for that. There is no substitute for human touch, contact, and physical comfort.

Last night I turned on some news again. I heard someone say that if we, as a country, had *shut down* just two weeks earlier, 90% of the lives we have lost so far, would have been saved. The ripple effect to the whole of mankind, to the planet, to our mental and physical health, to the levels of poverty and violence and neglect and starvation and suffering are all concepts none of us can begin to wrap our heads around.

Why get up in the morning? Because in my heart there lives the hope that I will hold my daughter again someday. In my heart lives the hope that she will hug me back with strong arms and that maybe *she* believes the cog in the wheel can be repaired.

Connect, Vote, and Don't Give Up
By Sara Williams

Born in 1943 in Marion, Indiana, Sara Williams
is a retired librarian, runs a business with her daughter,
and currently lives in Bozeman, Montana.

At 76 years old, I guess I qualify as an elder. I am honored. We live in a remote mountain location outside Bozeman, Montana. For over 40 years, we have lived in a modified form of isolation. But this is different. I am the main caregiver of my 92-year-old husband. My daughter and son-in-law live next to us. The "kids" have been able to keep us supplied with food and other essentials, which I am very thankful. Many in our age group feel vulnerable. I certainly do. I do venture out once in a while to go to the grocery store. This simple task has changed pretty dramatically for me. I have to formulate a strategy before I go to the store. Do I have my mask on correctly? Should I wear gloves while shopping, or is it enough to spray my hands with a disinfectant after leaving the store? I also miss dropping by a dear friend's house to give a hug and have a cup of tea.

So many strategies need to be in place when we leave our mountain house and plan for those face-to-face connections.

There are much broader implications and impact of this virus. It is not just the inconveniences that we face in our daily lives—most of us can handle that, but for many, it is far worse. I am thinking of the families that have lost loved ones; of those who have lost their jobs; the people who are in jeopardy of losing their homes, and losing needed services that were once in place, but have now evaporated; food no longer available for folks. The list goes on and on.

For most of us, this virus was totally unexpected. We have learned that our leadership was warned of the pandemic, but chose not to put a plan in place to counteract this deadly virus. What are the ramifications for the future? Will we have leadership in place that will have a plan when the next virus attacks? Can we make a moral choice to value people's lives and well-being over the financial interests of the few? Will our democracy survive? Will we ever be able to control racism in this country?

As an elder, I wish I knew the answers to these questions, but I don't have answers. I do have choices available to me. I can only think of what I can do personally to help effect change. First, keep informed on the issues and vote. Second, reach out to friends and family, and connect with them in compassionate way. Third, engage with others and talk about racism in this country, and discuss how we can face this moral challenge.

Racism is so serious and horrible that we must face our personal stereotypes and bigotries. Alone, hatred and fear can bring down our government.

This elder is not too optimistic. If our democracy survives, it will be changed and damaged for a long time. I feel very sad. I do feel fortunate to be able to connect with close friends and a loving family. My message: DON'T GIVE UP!

Create a New Normal
by Jill Woodworth

Born in 1953 in St. Charles, Illinois,
Jill Woodworth is a retired Nurse, Nurse Administrator,
Pilates and Gyrokinesis Instructor
and lives in Charleston, South Carolina.

When the stories about Wuhan and the outbreak of COVID-19 were new, I was concerned for our future in the United States. We have been warned for years that a pandemic like this was inevitable, yet we did little to prepare for it. People believed that this would never happen here. Now we are scrambling to catch up, instead of being ahead of the game.

My husband has multiple myeloma and has undergone three stem cell transplants. Having a spouse who has been seriously immuno-compromised for 11 years, this is not a new way of living in the world for us. My husband has worn N-95 masks whenever in stores, on airplanes, and always has a bottle of Purell in his pocket. He stays six feet away from others and only hugs me. I fear this virus would kill him. Now, except for bike rides and his weekly chemo treatments, he doesn't leave the house.

My daughter and I were wearing masks in the grocery store long before it was recommended. We were stared at for wearing them. Now people who aren't wearing masks are getting the stares. These days to minimize the risk to my husband, our daughter is the only one who does the shopping. Everything is wiped down before it enters the house. Even after she moves out in May, she will continue to shop for us.

We were preparing to list our home for sale and downsize. As the situation worsened in NYC we knew it would be coming here, if not already here. It was a stressful decision to make, but we pulled the listing. Although real estate is considered an essential business, we could not have people coming into the house. For us, the length of time between exposure and developing symptoms was very stressful. We self-quarantined weeks before the orders to stay-at-home were issued.

Exercise and long walks have helped to clear my head. A return to mindfulness meditation practice eases the stress. Reading, reconnecting with family via Zoom and phone calls, playing cribbage, watching (binging) Netflix and Amazon videos, have helped pass the time.

Initially, it was all the unknowns that were so frightening. I had days of low energy. I couldn't keep track of what day it was. The days all ran together. I stayed informed, but had to minimize the amount of news I heard. The stories were overwhelming. As people in our community started following the guidelines, I began to feel safer and more optimistic.

Currently, our Governor, Henry McMaster, is removing the stay-at-home order. This is a concern since our curve hasn't flattened. Our state does not have adequate testing, so the numbers aren't accurate. We aren't waiting for two weeks for the numbers to level off and I worry this may be moving too fast, too soon. We will see.

We are fortunate to be able to entertain ourselves, feed our family and our pets. We are retired on fixed incomes, so not experiencing the loss financially as so many others are.

I am frightened and sad for the healthcare professionals who go face to face with this everyday. Having been an ICU nurse, I can only imagine the stress this causes. I am grateful for all of those workers on the front lines. Grateful, as well, for all the essential workers who carry on through these unprecedented times.

I hope the world will be a better place when this is over. We are seeing the impact of humanity on the globe. The air is cleaner. The oceans, rivers, lakes, and even the canals in Venice are cleaner. Congestion and traffic is less. The environment has had a chance to heal through this. We shouldn't return to normal; we need to create a new normal. We must rethink the world. Rethink business as usual. Perhaps we can all live with a little less. Slow down the pace and appreciate one another in a new light.

As the restrictions are lifted, things won't dramatically change for my immediate family. We will continue to follow the CDC guidelines to protect ourselves and I may be the only one in the grocery store wearing a mask and gloves. We will not be safe until there is a vaccine. Eventually, we will list our home on the market, and get back to searching for our next home.

The world needs to be better prepared for this kind of event in the future. We MUST heed the warnings and be more proactive rather, than reactive.

Meanwhile, it is spring. Beautiful sunny days. I am enjoying sitting out on the porch smelling the jasmine blossoms and listening to the birds.

Pandemic Priorities
by Tracy Woodworth

Born in 1956 in Pasadena, California,
Tracy Woodworth is a retired Legal Assistant
and lives in Eden, Utah.

In late January, I was visiting my mom in Minnesota when news of the Coronavirus disease was coming out of China. In my hotel room, I watched the local news folks on TV questioning each other about this strange outbreak. On Facebook, I recall someone joking about a new, potent cocktail made with Corona beer and " Lyme juice." The virus was, just another Asian disease, not something that would become a problem for us.

My husband and I live in Utah and I have been in "quarantine" since March 16. We retired two years ago, and our lives haven't been affected drastically, since we aren't big socializers, financially we're fine, our health is good, we can keep hiking and walking with the dogs. We are able to get all the groceries, prescriptions, and libations that we need. The weather has turned to a beautiful warm spring and we can sit out back with a glass of wine and a fire on cool evenings while we read or play cribbage. We are extremely lucky and cherish everyday we stay well.

We have been planning a move—a major one—out of Utah and back to where I grew up in Minnesota. We both have been here 40+ years and are ready for a change of scenery with a bigger house, more cultural options, and a better view out the back window. We are tired of the bad air that comes with the winter inversion. Tired of the horrible traffic and the crowds moving in. Tired of our small downtown turning into a loud, cramped city with more and more massive apartments squeezing in on every block. We are getting older and we want a change before we die.

And suddenly in the last two months our perspectives have shifted and I recognize the biggest impact the pandemic has had on me are that the things we had been constantly whining about aren't so bad anymore. The pollution is almost gone as the traffic has subsided significantly. The I-15 Freeway is a breeze to drive, almost pleasant. Downtown Salt Lake is quiet and easy to get around. Crime is down, and "porch pirates" are virtually non-existent since residents are pretty much home all day to guard their deliveries. Even shopping at Costco is a snap with minimal crowds and short checkout lines.

But most significantly has been our realization of how important human contact and friendship is. We walk the neighborhood with our dogs like we always have, but now we notice how many more people are doing the same, and even behind their masks we can see them greeting us with their eyes. Everyone is craving socialization—a wave or a smile—and those who were strangers to us before are becoming friends. The feeling of community and need for interaction has become paramount. And it's something I don't think we could find by moving to a new place. In uncertain times, we need to hang on to what we're certain of. We really do have a solid base here and more friends and stability than we ever realized. We can still find a new house with a better view, but we don't need to move so far away to find it. Growing old isn't bad, but growing old without friends and familiar territory sounds as hard as quarantine and isolation.

My priorities have changed. Things I thought I needed aren't high on my list anymore. I haven't spent much money buying *stuff* besides groceries and pet supplies. The little things are the biggest now—friends, neighbors, nature, clean air, solitude. Certainly a lot of this might be temporary, but who knows? If we could keep it this simple would that be all bad? At this point there isn't a definitive future for me. It's hard to plan much these days beyond a trip to the market or the garden store.

It's early May, now. My mom died of natural causes ten days after

I visited her and just before the virus started spreading in the United States. For years mom had been praying to die in her sleep, as her "non-quality" of life had become almost unbearable. Her timing was impeccable: the assisted-living facility she lived in was closed down permanently a few weeks ago due to staff and administrators contracting the virus and unable to care for residents. I miss her immensely every day, but I am so glad she made her exit when she did.

And life goes on. I believe we will get through this, bumps and all, if we play by the rules. I hope so.